T0372452

OUTPLAYED

Also by
David Lockwood

Fooled by the Winners:
How Survivor Bias Deceives Us

OUTPLAYED

How Game Theory Is Used Against Us

DAVID LOCKWOOD

GREENLEAF
BOOK GROUP PRESS

Published by Greenleaf Book Group Press
Austin, Texas
www.gbgpress.com

Distributed by Greenleaf Book Group

For ordering information or special discounts for bulk purchases, please
contact Greenleaf Book Group at PO Box 91869, Austin, TX 78709,
512.891.6100.

Design and composition by Greenleaf Book Group
Cover design by Greenleaf Book Group
Cover Image: ©Getty/Image Source

Publisher's Cataloging-in-Publication data is available.

Print ISBN: 978-1-62634-979-7

eBook ISBN: 978-1-62634-980-3

Part of the Tree Neutral® program, which offsets the number of trees
consumed in the production and printing of this book by taking proactive
steps, such as planting trees in direct proportion to the number of trees
used: www.treeneutral.com

TreeNeutral

Printed in the United States of America on acid-free paper

22 23 24 25 26 27 28 29   10 9 8 7 6 5 4 3 2 1

First Edition

To my family

*Many people find the concept of
"mutual homicide"—or mutual assured
destruction—very comforting.*

—HERMAN KAHN, *Thinking About the
Unthinkable in the 1980s*

*If you've been in the (poker) game
30 minutes and you don't know who
the patsy is, you're the patsy.*

—WARREN BUFFETT, 1987 Berkshire
Hathaway Letter to Shareholders

CONTENTS

Doomsday Machines, Prisoners, and TV Remotes

Perimeter and Mutual Assured Destruction

The Russians call it Mertvaya Ruka, or Dead Hand. Among security analysts, it is known as Perimeter.

Perimeter is a defense system that monitors radiation levels, seismic activities, and air pressure around Moscow. If it determines Moscow has been destroyed by nuclear weapons, the system will contact the war room of the Soviet General Staff. If there is no response, Perimeter will assume that the Soviet leadership has been vaporized and transfer control of all Soviet nuclear weapons to a special group of Soviet Air Force officers living inside a bunker buried deep in the Ural Mountains. These officers have instructions to immediately launch the Russian fleet of intercontinental ballistic missiles and incinerate the 332 million residents of the United States.

Built during the Cold War, Perimeter remains in operation today.

Perimeter is a real-world example of game theory in action. Russia, the United States, and the rest of the world would be better off without thousands of missiles bristling with nuclear warheads poised in silos and fueled for launch, ready to slaughter the inhabitants of entire nations with the press of a button. But no major nation is willing to disarm for fear it will be left defenseless. And so the nuclear powers of the world spend hundreds of billions of dollars each year on atomic weapons that threaten the survival of life on Earth.

Game Theory

Game theory is fundamentally about strategy and thus has applications far beyond poker, chess, or checkers. It guides us on when to cooperate and when to compete. It shows us how to structure incentives to get others to work with us. It explains why nations such as Russia and the United States adopt policies that are individually rational and collectively crazy.

Game theory has a long history. In 1 Kings, the Bible tells of how King Solomon employed game theory to determine who was the mother of an infant. During the fifth century BC, Sun Tzu advised on when to engage enemy forces in *The Art of War*. Later that century, Thucydides suggested schemes to defeat neighboring Greek city-states in *History of the Peloponnesian War*. But these formulations of game theory offered non-numerical strategies applicable to a specific set of circumstances.

As a formal branch of mathematics, game theory would have to wait another twenty-five hundred years for two geniuses: John von Neumann and John Nash. In 1928, von Neumann was the first to demonstrate that a numerical strategy could be deduced from mathematical axioms for general types of games.[1] In 1949,

Nash extended von Neumann's work to include the social and life sciences. Together, they created a new set of tools, consisting of axioms, proofs, and equations, with which to plot strategy across a wide variety of fields.

These tools can be used against us—or they can be deployed to our advantage. Armed with a knowledge of game theory, there is no reason to be outplayed by others.

About This Book

Many books and articles have been published on game theory, but most have been inaccessible because of the high level of mathematical fluency required. But there are no equations or proofs to be found here. This book is about application, not theory. While the math behind game theory is sometimes difficult to grasp, lessons can be learned from analyzing concrete flesh-and-blood examples that can be understood and used by anyone.

This book is also not about parlor games. Many excellent texts explain how to win at everything from Monopoly to mah-jongg. This is not one of them. Instead, we focus on the application of game theory to broader topics, such as political science, economics, and biology.

We start with examples of game theory from before the modern era, then move on to the work of von Neumann and Nash and their take on the prisoner's dilemma, a well-known paradox. Next, we tackle evolution, conventional and nuclear war, the administration of justice, and relationships. We also analyze elections, auctions, and financial markets. We even develop strategies to gain access to the TV remote from the love of your life.

Before von Neumann and Nash laid the foundations of modern game theory, numerous books and papers were written about strategy, but they lacked general principles, formulas, or numerical solutions. While filled with instructive examples, these texts were a series of ad hoc observations but offered conflicting advice due to their anecdotal nature. Among these texts is the first known written account of the use of game theory.

It concerns a snake and an apple.

CHAPTER 1

Early Game Theory: Conflicting Advice

Adam and Eve: A Really Bad Outcome (for All of Us)

In Genesis 2:17, God says: "But of the tree of knowledge of good and evil, thou shalt not eat of it: for in the day that thou eatest thereof thou shalt surely die."

This prohibition was not a problem until Eve had a conversation with a snake who promised that just a bite and "ye shall be as God."[1] After Eve shared this new piece of information with her husband, the two became suspicious about what they had been previously told. Maybe God didn't want them to eat from the forbidden tree because they would become gods themselves. In all their walks with Him in the Garden of Eden, God had failed to mention that the source of His powers was fruit.

But finding out the real story had a big potential downside: God had promised to summarily execute anyone who broke His one commandment to date. Even if what the snake said was true, it was better to be an alive human than a dead god. So Adam and Eve employed some game theory to get what they wanted.

For God to make good on his threat, He would have to kill them and start all over again. But God could reasonably assume that Adam and Eve 2.0 and subsequent versions would similarly be unable to resist the temptation to eat of the tree of knowledge. God would then realize that if He killed them, He would find Himself in a blood-soaked endless cycle of double murder, a heavenly serial killer exterminating generation after generation of His creations. Adam and Eve deduced that a series of multiple homicides was not the story line God had envisioned for the first chapters of Genesis.

Adam and Eve were also aware that God could kill them and create a new and improved First Couple without free will. This would avoid the need to snuff out subsequent generations of His creations. But then God would have to admit to having made a big mistake the first time. Once again, not a good start to the narrative of the Bible about a supreme being who could do no wrong.

So Adam and Eve cleverly surmised that even if they followed the snake's advice, God would back down and choose a lesser punishment. In fact, that is exactly what He did. After Adam and Eve disobeyed God, He reduced the penalty for breaking His only commandment from summary execution to banishment. According to biblical tradition, Adam and Eve went on to live for many centuries afterward.

But everyone was worse off in the end. Adam and Eve had to move out. God would go on to suffer many years of disappointments. In retrospect, nobody liked how things worked out. If Adam and Eve had followed just one simple dietary restriction,

God's sole ask, then the overall outcome might have been better for all concerned.

For God's part, He could have created a tree of knowledge in which the forbidden fruit was poisonous. This would have eliminated the ability for Him to change His mind. Then Adam and Eve would have been confronted with a stark choice: an uncertain chance they could become gods or certain death. There would no longer be the option for Adam and Eve to back God into a corner, forcing Him to renege on His commitment to capital punishment. If God had structured the first incentives differently, then we all might still be enjoying a life of leisure.

The author of Genesis is illustrating the calamitous and long-lasting consequences of failing to cooperate, in this case with God. But another example later in the Bible comes to a different conclusion about whether cooperation is the best strategy.

Solomon's Judgment: Give and Take

In 1 Kings 3:16–28 (New King James Version), the Bible tells us that two women presented themselves to King Solomon, each claiming to be the mother of an infant. To determine the real mother, King Solomon commanded his guards to "divide the living child in two, and give half to one and half to the other." The first woman to speak cried, "O my lord, give her the living child, and by no means kill him!" Then the second woman said, "Let him be neither mine nor yours, but divide him."

King Solomon had his answer and gave the child to the first woman.

This was the right outcome. But the second woman was outplayed. With some basic understanding of game theory, she could have outplayed the king.

If the second woman had accepted the baby, then King Solomon would have had no way to determine who the real mother was.

The "wise" king would not have known whether the fake mother had spoken first and then the real mother accepted the infant, or whether the real mother had spoken first and then the fake mother dishonestly took the child.

If King Solomon had understood some basic game theory, then he would have structured the choices for the two women differently. Instead of imminent infanticide, the king could have offered custody of the child in exchange for a lifetime of servitude. If both had accepted the king's offer, then the women would share the job of raising the child. Given these choices, the real mother would have accepted the offer: an outcome of even shared custody of her child would have been worth serving the king for the rest of her life. The fake mother would have rejected the offer: the joys of jointly raising another woman's child would have been less than the cost of a lifetime of servitude.

The Bible does not record how many successors to the throne of David followed King Solomon's example and threatened to carve up babies. But some knowledge from game theory about how to structure incentives would have enabled King Solomon and generations of subsequent rulers to avoid imperiling the lives of infants.

The author of 1 Kings seems be suggesting that the lesson we should draw from Solomon's judgment is that the fake mother should not have cooperated when playing King Solomon's game—she should have lied about her true intentions.

Around the same time 1 Kings was written, a Chinese general on the other side of the world also recommended against cooperation.

Sun Tzu: An Infinite Variety of Ways to Deceive

Sun Tzu is believed to have written *The Art of War* in the fifth century BC.[2] The book contains thirteen chapters devoted to military strategy and tactics. It has been a favorite text for military leaders from Mao Zedong to Norman Schwarzkopf.

The depth of the analysis and the level of sophistication in *The Art of War* are quite remarkable. Compare *The Art of War* and a similarly highly revered work, *On War* by Carl von Clausewitz, written some twenty-five hundred years later. Clausewitz believed in total war and the importance of overwhelming force to achieve victory. As Clausewitz declared in one of his famous dictums, "To introduce into the philosophy of war a principle of moderation would be an absurdity—war is an act of violence pushed to its utmost bounds."[3] In *On War*, Clausewitz counseled crushing the opposing army by throwing more men and materials into battle.

By contrast, Sun Tzu wrote that "the supreme art of war is to subdue the enemy without fighting."[4] The mathematics underlying Sun Tzu's ideas had not yet been developed, but he nevertheless stressed the importance of following a mixed rather than a pure strategy.[5] We will discuss the differences between the two in Chapter 6, but the short version is that a pure strategy is consistent, whereas a mixed strategy is unpredictable and therefore often more effective. In an analogy from poker, bluffing all the time doesn't work. Sun Tzu believed you should be unpredictable to keep opposing generals from discerning your real strategy. He wrote, "Although everyone can see the outward aspect, none understands the way in which I have created victory. Therefore, when I have won a victory, I do not repeat my tactics but respond to circumstances in an infinite variety of ways."[6] The phrase "an infinite variety of ways" suggests Sun Tzu was referring to the modern concept of randomness, which, as we will see, plays a critical role in modern game theory when constructing mixed strategies.

While Sun Tzu wrote of a mixed strategy based on randomness more than two thousand years before this idea was formalized in game theory, he did not believe in the benefits of pursuing peace. For this ancient Chinese strategist, there was no common ground to be found with the enemy. He believed opposing generals would lie, cheat, and steal to achieve victory, regardless of whatever agreements or promises were made.

For Sun Tzu, cooperation was not an option. At about the same time, a famous Greek general came to the same conclusion.

Thucydides: Take No Prisoners

Thucydides was an Athenian general who wrote *History of the Peloponnesian War*, a contemporary account of hostilities between Sparta and Athens during the fifth century BC. Numerous aspects of game theory are related to the battles between these two city-states, but let's focus on the most famous, which is contained in the Melian Dialogue.[7]

The Athenian empire comprised Athens and neighboring cities that had either been annexed or were allied. Given the breadth of their empire, the Athenians did not have enough ships or soldiers to subjugate all the cities they had conquered or had committed to defend. When the annexed island of Melos revolted, Athens had to decide whether to retaliate by killing the men and selling the women as slaves or executing only the top government officials.

Some in the Athenian Assembly argued that executing all the Melian men would serve no military purpose, as the Melians were too few to pose a threat to Athens. It was also argued that demonstrating a willingness to cooperate with the defeated Melians would send the right message to other allied cities. However, most in the assembly thought this would be exactly the wrong message, and the Athenians promptly dispatched an army to carry out the harsher punishment.

Putting aside the moral issues, Thucydides sides with the view that signaling a willingness not to cooperate is the more effective strategy, even after the battle is won. Thucydides was steeped in the prevailing wisdom in the Greek world at that time: might makes right, and cooperation is not the natural or preferred choice.

As seen from these examples, the consensus in the ancient world was that working with others was not the preferred option. By contrast, most strategists in the modern world have decidedly come down on the side of cooperation.

David Hume: Two Farmers

David Hume published *A Treatise of Human Nature*, one of the most important works in Western philosophy, in two installments in 1739 and 1740. The *Treatise* sets out the Scottish philosopher's views on a wide variety of topics, including empiricism, atheism, skepticism, free will, and personal identity. Hume was also the first to explicitly call out issues related to cooperation in a form comparable to the prisoner's dilemma, which we discuss in Chapter 2. In the *Treatise*, Hume describes what has come to be known as the farmers' game:

> *Your corn is ripe to-day; mine will be so tomorrow. 'Tis profitable for us both, that I shou'd labour with you to-day, and that you shou'd aid me to-morrow. I have no kindness for you, and know you have as little for me. I will not, therefore, take any pains on your account; and shou'd I labour with you upon my own account, in expectation of a return, I know I shou'd be disappointed, and that I shou'd in vain depend upon your gratitude. Here then I leave you to labour alone: You treat me in the same manner. The seasons change; and both of us lose our harvests for want of mutual confidence and security.*[8]

In this case, the right strategy seems to be not to cooperate. A farmer reasons that another farmer will renege on his promise once the first farmer has helped bring in that farmer's crop. The second farmer reasons similarly. Therefore, neither farmer helps the other, and both farmers in the end are worse off.

In practice, Hume observed that farmers regularly help each other out, and he believed this was due to "convention."[9] But Hume does not explain how this convention started in the first place, as initially there would have been no social norm. In addition, Hume does not offer an explanation as to how this convention could be sustained. A farmer would have an incentive to call in sick on the harvest day of his neighbors, and this "flu" would soon spread throughout an agricultural community.

Hume favored cooperation but offered no reason why cooperation would be a prevalent strategy. His advice seems to have been to try to join a community of farmers in which the long-standing custom was to be a good neighbor.

Hume's main intellectual rival at the time had a very different solution to this dilemma.

Jean-Jacques Rousseau: A Stag and a Hare

In 1755, Jean-Jacques Rousseau composed the *Discourse on Inequality*, in which the French philosopher laid out what he saw as the evils of civil society. One of those evils is that humans in civil society are unable to reason together and therefore do not cooperate.

Rousseau used a game he called the "stag hunt" to illustrate people's inability to come together and arrive at a mutually beneficial outcome:

> *If it was a matter of hunting a deer, everyone well realized that he must remain faithful to his post; but if a hare happened to pass within reach of one of them, we cannot doubt that he would have gone off in pursuit of it without scruple.*[10]

While not explicit, the assumption behind Rousseau's example is that it takes at least two hunters to take down a stag but only one to snag a hare. The best outcome for two or more hunters is to cooperate and hunt the stag together. But the hunter who pursues the stag alone will come back with nothing. The hunter who chooses to pursue a hare will at least be guaranteed something to eat. Therefore, to their mutual disadvantage, hunters chase rabbits.

Rousseau viewed the resolution of the stag hunt through the lens of his theory that uncorrupted morals persist in a state of nature. Rousseau is famously quoted as saying, "Men are wicked, but man is good." Rousseau thought the way to resolve the dilemma posed by the stag hunt was to radically reform civil society, the primary cause of human conflict. Once society had been reformed, everyone would hunt together, and soon there would be a surplus of stag meat.

Rousseau's proposed solution seems to be neither to cooperate nor to compete but to do a hard reset on society, returning to something akin to a state of nature. Although appealing in theory, returning to Rousseau's version of the Garden of Eden would be difficult in practice.

Some eight decades later, another Frenchman would offer a more realistic solution.

Antoine Cournot: French Spring Water

In 1838, the French mathematician and economist Antoine Cournot identified issues with cooperation in his treatise *Researches into the Mathematical Principles of the Theory of Wealth*. In this work, Cournot analyzed the duopoly held by the two companies that controlled the market for French spring water. He expected the two firms to conspire to maintain prices at near-monopoly-high levels, given their combined market power. However, he observed that the two firms regularly competed with each other on price.

This has become known as an example of Cournot competition, which has been applied to modern cartels, such as OPEC (the Organization of the Petroleum Exporting Countries). Cournot demonstrated that there are incentives to lower prices and not cooperate. The best outcome to maximize profits for both firms would be to severely limit production of French spring water. However, Cournot found that the firms could not resist the temptation to produce more than the profit-maximizing output. By not cooperating, both parties suffered in the form of lower profits.

Unlike Hume and Rousseau, Cournot talked about the possibility of a state of equilibrium in which the two producers use trial and error to converge on the quantities of French spring water that should be bottled to maximize profits for both. With this formulation, Cournot got a lot closer than those who had come before to a strategy that could be applied broadly. In fact, Cournot described the basic idea that John Nash would write about 111 years later in his 1949 doctoral thesis. But Cournot did not offer mathematical proofs or a means to quantify his solution.

While these examples are compelling stories, they are just that—anecdotal examples in which some advised cooperation and others recommended against it. Despite these differences, there is one common thread: individual and collective interests are not aligned. In the examples above, the payoffs differ in each case, but the overall outcome is the same: the average individual is worse off in the absence of cooperation.

In modern life, we often cooperate with others. Motorists (almost) universally agree to drive on one side of the road. By agreeing to keep either to the left or right, depending on the country in question, drivers and their passengers are more likely to arrive safely at their destination. Railroads compete furiously for customers yet still agree to build the same width of track. Other examples of cooperation range from a common currency to a common language. On the other hand, we also regularly decide to compete for jobs, schools, mates, and parking spaces.

So how can we determine when to cooperate—and when to compete?

That was the question John von Neumann and John Nash sought to answer.

CHAPTER 2

The Prisoner's Dilemma: It Was the Other Guy

John von Neumann: The Theory of (All) Games

John von Neumann (1903–1957) was a Hungarian mathematician who came to America to escape the Nazis.[1] Before his untimely death at age fifty-three, von Neumann made fundamental breakthroughs in mathematics, physics, chemistry, economics, computing, and cybernetics. He published more than 150 papers in scientific journals during his lifetime. In addition to his theoretical work, he made significant contributions in the applied sciences. He predicted how cells replicate before Watson and Crick discovered the structure of DNA. He was one of the most important contributors to the Manhattan Project.

Von Neumann held significant government positions and influenced postwar military and energy policies. He was an advisor to Presidents Truman and Eisenhower and to cabinet secretaries of both administrations. He worked for the RAND Corporation on US military strategy and helped formulate the doctrine of mutual assured destruction (MAD). He was a leading member of the first Atomic Energy Commission, warned of the dangers of global warming caused by the burning of fossil fuels, and predicted the development of artificial intelligence.

Besides his extraordinary intelligence, von Neumann was well liked by most people with whom he had contact. This accounted for his success in working with teams of scientists as well as national political leaders. Tragically, von Neumann was felled at an early age by cancer. Evidence of his prominent position as a scientist and advisor to presidents is that in his last days von Neumann was guarded by military security at the hospital, lest he reveal state secrets while heavily medicated.

Throughout his life, von Neumann was an avid poker player. He and his wife, Klara, frequently held parties at their house with others from the Institute for Advanced Study at Princeton, where von Neumann was a fellow with leading scientists and mathematicians such as Albert Einstein and Kurt Gödel. By all accounts, von Neumann played poker "not terribly well."[2] He thought that he could increase his winnings by developing an optimal strategy for bluffing, based on mathematical principles. In 1928, he published a paper in German, "Zur Theorie der Gesellschaftsspiele," which translates to "On the Theory of Parlor Games."[3] In this paper, an outgrowth of his efforts to improve his poker playing, von Neumann proved there was an optimal strategy for two-person zero-sum games. With this breakthrough, he established game theory as a new branch of mathematics.

However, virtually nobody understood the importance of this discovery, including von Neumann. After he published the paper, von Neumann returned to pure mathematics and physics and forgot about researching what, in his mind, were just table games.

More than a decade later, Oskar Morgenstern, an economist at Princeton, read von Neumann's 1928 article and realized its significance. In 1940, he drafted an academic paper that applied von Neumann's theory of parlor games to problems in economics and approached von Neumann to discuss it. Von Neumann's response was to suggest they write a book together. Over the next four years, the two men expanded Morgenstern's paper to 641 pages of dense equations and extended proofs. Their book was published in 1944 as *Theory of Games and Economic Behavior*, and von Neumann's 1928 discovery was catapulted from the small world of table games to the big world of economics.

The reaction to the book was immediate. The *New York Times* ran a front-page story titled "Mathematical Theory of Poker Is Applied to Business Problems: Gaming Strategy Used in Economics."[4] For centuries, economists worked largely by induction, poring over large sets of data to identify consistent patterns that could be codified into economic laws. After von Neumann and Morgenstern's book was published, many believed that economics could now rely on deductions from mathematical axioms to make predictions about human behavior and that the rigorous mathematics of game theory would yield more accurate economic forecasts. There was hope that this could be the dawn of a new age for the social sciences in general and economics in particular.

But von Neumann and Morgenstern's work only proved that there was an optimal strategy for two-person zero-sum games, although they did discuss other types of games at length. Most interactions in the social sciences and economics are among more than two people, and cooperation typically yields outcomes that are non-zero sum. For example, a marketplace for an exchange of goods is typically characterized by more than two parties, in which all are better off after transacting.

To apply game theory more broadly required expanding

beyond two individuals in which one person's gain was another person's loss. Hence, after the initial euphoria, most economists and social scientists lost interest in game theory. *Theory of Games* and *Economic Behavior* had been published to great fanfare. Yet, within several years, the book was largely forgotten, read mainly by those concerned with military strategy and certain areas within operational research.[5]

It took the genius of John Nash to revive game theory.

John Nash: A Beautiful and Troubled Mind

John Forbes Nash Jr. (1928–2015) was an American mathematician who made fundamental discoveries in game theory and geometry.[6] He is best known for the "Nash equilibrium," which proved that there is at least one optimal strategy for many types of games, such as the prisoner's dilemma. Because of the sheer breadth and impact of his work, Nash has been called "the most remarkable mathematician of the second half of the [twentieth] century."[7] Nash was an advanced student at an early age. At nineteen, he earned a bachelor's and master's degree in mathematics from Carnegie Mellon University and at twenty-two a PhD in mathematics from Princeton with his dissertation "Non-Cooperative Games," which outlined what has become known as the Nash equilibrium. At the same time, he submitted a one-page proof of the Nash equilibrium to the National Academy of Sciences. These two papers would later earn him a Nobel Prize.

In 1951, after graduating from Princeton, Nash joined the mathematics faculty of the Massachusetts Institute of Technology (MIT), where he remained until 1959. While at MIT, the RAND Corporation hired Nash as a part-time consultant with a high-level security clearance to work on the implications of game theory for US nuclear strategy. But Nash was fired from RAND in 1954 after he was arrested at 2:00 a.m. on a Santa Monica beach during a sting operation that targeted gay men. RAND arranged for the charges to be dropped and the records expunged from police files in the interest of national security.[8]

In 1955, Nash wrote a series of letters to the National Security Agency (NSA) in which he proposed encryption techniques based on computational hardness. He also outlined the architecture for the first parallel processing computer. Both suggestions were ignored by the NSA. Today, Nash's ideas are the basis for parts of modern cryptography and the design of microchips.

Several years later, Nash began to exhibit signs of mental illness. His wife reported signs of paranoia: Nash believed all men with red ties were part of a communist plot against him. He told people he was receiving encrypted messages from inhabitants of another galaxy, and he would soon become the Emperor of Antarctica.[9] As a consequence, Nash was involuntarily committed to McLean Hospital, the mental health facility of Harvard Medical School, and diagnosed with "paranoid schizophrenia, brought on by latent homosexuality," which at the time was cruelly considered a mental disorder.[10] After fifty days of confinement, he was released.

Nash promptly resigned his position as a professor, outraged that MIT had allowed him to be committed against his will. Nash and his wife moved to Princeton, but his behavior became increasingly bizarre and he was once again involuntarily committed at a local sanitarium. He underwent insulin shock therapy, which Nash would later describe as "torture."[11] After his release, Nash got divorced and fled to Europe, and for the next decade he moved back and forth between the two continents and in and out of mental institutions.

In 1970, Nash decided he would no longer seek treatment for his mental illnesses and moved in as a paying boarder in his ex-wife's house in Princeton. He was allowed by the university to audit courses, and Nash's life began to return to some normalcy.

While he did not formally teach, Nash often attended events at the university and would speak at length with students. He became known as the "Phantom of Fine Hall" because he sometimes walked the corridors of various Princeton buildings late at night scribbling lengthy equations on blackboards.[12]

In 1994, Nash was awarded the Nobel Prize in economics for a "pioneering analysis of equilibria in the theory of non-cooperative games."[13] He had not held an academic post or published a scientific paper since 1959.[14] The Nobel Prize gave Nash a renewed sense of purpose, and his symptoms dissipated with the passing years. He remarried his former wife in 2001.

In 2015, Nash and his wife traveled to Oslo, where Nash received the Abel Prize, an award given annually by the King of Norway to an outstanding mathematician. As they returned home, their taxi struck a guardrail. Nash and his wife were ejected from the car and killed instantly.

The Nash Equilibrium: A "Trivial" Idea

Nash had read von Neumann and Morgenstern's work and thought there might be a way to expand their theories to multiple individuals and non-zero-sum games. In 1949, Nash went to see von Neumann in his office at Princeton to discuss whether Nash should pursue this idea. At that time, von Neumann was one of the most famous mathematicians and scientists in the world and an advisor to the US president. Nash was an unknown PhD student.

Von Neumann motioned Nash into his office, and Nash began to explain how to extend von Neumann's work. Before Nash could finish, von Neumann interrupted him and dismissed him from his office with a wave of his hand and the comment, "That's trivial, you know."[15]

Nash was deeply hurt and never approached von Neumann again. He channeled his anger into intense work on a theory of games that included non-zero-sum games involving more than two parties. From this he produced his Princeton PhD dissertation and the one-page proof of the Nash equilibrium that would earn him a Nobel Prize. The Nash equilibrium demonstrated for the first time that there was at least one optimal strategy for any finite multiple-person non-zero-sum game. Because of Nash's discovery, the mathematics of game theory could now be broadly applied to economics and the social sciences.

The Nash equilibrium has several features that are especially useful when trying to model behavior in the real world.

One has been called the "announcement test." In a Nash equilibrium, even if all players announced their strategies to each other at the same time, none of them would make a different decision. If this were not the case, then an announcement of a player's strategy would cause other players to also change their strategy, resulting in cascading rounds of new strategies and an unstable equilibrium. By contrast, a Nash equilibrium is stable, a fixed point around which all players will rationally converge because it is the best strategy for each individual acting in their own self-interest, even in hindsight.

A Nash equilibrium can also be established without players entering into agreements with each other, either through communication or by forming alliances. In terms of the nomenclature of game theory, a Nash equilibrium is non-cooperative, meaning that players act independently and do not work with other players or rely on an external third party to enforce agreements. Therefore, a Nash equilibrium has the property of being self-reinforcing. In that way, a Nash equilibrium is comparable to the invisible hand postulated by Adam Smith: participants in a market arrive at a stable equilibrium point without entering into explicit agreements with each other. But Smith assumed the resulting equilibrium, the product of supply and demand, would be the best outcome for all.

Nash demonstrated the opposite: the outcome of a Nash equilibrium, while optimal for each individual, was worse for the group as a whole.

But because it directly contradicted the conventional wisdom at the time, Nash's work was immediately called into question.

RAND and the Prisoner's Dilemma

RAND is a military think tank, headquartered in Santa Monica, California. Founded in 1948 and initially funded by the Air Force, RAND brought together many of the leading mathematicians, economists, and scientists in the United States during the Cold War. The main task of RAND in the 1950s and early 1960s was to develop strategies to combat the threat of nuclear war. Out of this work at RAND came what has become known as the prisoner's dilemma.

In 1950, when Nash first arrived at RAND, the twenty-two-year-old mathematician was asked to advise Merrill Flood and Melvin Dresher, two established RAND researchers almost twenty years his senior, on game theory. Nash was recognized as a kind of boy genius and one of the pioneers in this new branch of mathematics. In his PhD thesis, Nash had presented six "simple examples" to illustrate his theory, and what is labeled "Ex. 2" is an example of the prisoner's dilemma. But, as was typical of Nash, he had attached no labels to the numbers and had given no intuitive explanations. He simply noted that Ex. 2 had the Strong Solution (b, B), which in the notation he employed meant that the optimal strategy was for neither party to cooperate. None of the other five examples in his PhD thesis exhibited this characteristic.

Flood and Dresher decided to empirically test Nash's solution to Ex. 2. In January 1950, they conducted an experiment, which they labeled "A Non-Cooperative Pair," to test the willingness of two individuals to cooperate. The payoffs were varying amounts of pennies,[16] and the players were two fellow researchers at RAND,

Armen Alchian and John Williams. The game was repeated one hundred times, which is probably why they used pennies.[17]

At that time, Albert Tucker, a professor at Princeton, was visiting his friend Dresher at RAND and saw an outline of their experiment on a blackboard.[18] Tucker was a professor of mathematics at Princeton and had been Nash's PhD thesis advisor. Hence, Tucker would have recognized the outlines of Nash's Ex. 2 scribbled in chalk. Tucker was in California because he was on sabbatical at Stanford University during the 1949–1950 school year. As part of his sabbatical, he was required to teach a course in psychology. In May 1950, Tucker gave his students at Stanford some handouts that outlined the paradox of what he called "the prisoner's dilemma."

Tucker did not express payoffs in pennies like Flood and Merrill but instead used an intuitive example to illustrate Nash's Ex. 2:

> *Two men, charged with a joint violation of law, are held separately by the police. Each is told that (1) if one confesses and the other does not, the former will be given a reward . . . and the latter will be given a large fine . . . (2) if both confess, each will be given a small fine. . . . At the same time each has good reason to believe that (3) if neither confesses, both will go clear.*[19]

In Tucker's example, you get a reward or a small fine by confessing. You get nothing or a large fine by not confessing. Hence, you should always confess. Both players will reason similarly; therefore, both will confess, and both will pay a small fine. However, the best outcome for the two of them is for neither to confess so that both avoid paying any fine at all.

This outcome was quite different from the prevailing

conventional wisdom in economics at that time. Up to this point, economists believed the best way to maximize the overall welfare of a society was for individuals to act in their own self-interest. The implicit assumption was that an "invisible hand" (a term first coined by economist Adam Smith) guided economic behavior to produce outcomes that were, on average, best for all. Nash had just shown the opposite: when individuals act in their own best interests, the group as a whole suffers.

But it was worse than that: Nash was not making an empirical observation about how most people behave in real life. Rather, Nash claimed that he had used mathematics to prove that the optimal strategy in the case of the prisoner's dilemma was to never cooperate. Nash was not the first to point out that cooperation may not be the optimal strategy. However, he was the first to prove mathematically that in many games, such as the prisoner's dilemma, cooperation was a losing proposition for an individual player. This result shook the foundations of economics and several other social sciences.

An Experiment and an Unexpected Outcome

Flood and Dresher, the two older, established RAND researchers, were familiar with the PhD thesis of the much younger "hotshot" recent Princeton graduate. Recall that when deciding to test Nash's theory, Flood and Dresher named the experiment with pennies "A Non-Cooperative Pair," a direct reference to the title of Nash's thesis.

When the RAND researchers tabulated the results of the experiment with pennies played by their colleagues, they found an unexpected outcome: a Nash equilibrium was only rarely achieved. The Nash equilibrium in the prisoner's dilemma is to never cooperate. In fact, Alchian and Williams, the two RAND researchers, cooperated most of the time. Of the one hundred rounds of the pennies game, the Nash equilibrium occurred only fourteen times, the scenario in which both failed to cooperate. One player cooperated and the other did not twenty-six times, and the most common outcome was that both cooperated, which occurred sixty times.[20] Despite the fact that Nash had mathematically proven that not cooperating was the optimal strategy, the experiment showed that in practice players cooperated more often than not.

Nash was not happy with these results. The experiment seemed to demonstrate that his theory did not represent human behavior in the real world. At first, Nash reacted emotionally and wrote to Flood and Dresher that the results were the fault of the players: "It is really striking, however, how inefficient AA and JW were in obtaining the rewards. One would have thought them more rational."[21]

Flood responded diplomatically on behalf of himself and his colleagues: "Dr. Dresher and I were glad to receive these comments . . . even though we would not change our interpretation of the experiment along the line indicated by Dr. Nash."[22]

Nash then wrote more objectively that the flaw in this experiment as a test of equilibrium point theory is that the experiment really amounts to having the players play one large multi-move game. . . . It's fairly clear that one should expect an approximation to this behavior . . . to test the opponent's mettle during the game.[23]

In fact, Nash was right, although not about the rationality of the players. What the experiment showed was that when a game is played multiple times, players learn to cooperate.

In the pennies game, each player "punished" the other player in the next round if that player failed to cooperate in the previous round. After repeated rounds, the players began to cooperate, and then this pattern was largely sustained over time. In the first fifty rounds, the two RAND researchers cooperated 42 percent of the time, but in the last fifty rounds that number rose to 80 percent.

After reviewing the results of the Flood and Dresher

experiments, Nash realized that an iterated game may have a different outcome than a game played just once. Nash concluded that cooperation in the present depended on an expectation of cooperation in the future.

Conclusions

The question of when to cooperate is at the heart of game theory. Von Neumann proved in his 1928 paper that there is an optimal strategy for a given zero-sum two-person game and expanded the concept with Morgenstern in their 1944 book. Nash then showed there was an optimal strategy for non-zero-sum games involving more than two parties. This allowed the mathematics of game theory to be applied more broadly to the social and life sciences.

The Flood and Dresher experiment demonstrated that iterated games can have a very different outcome than those played only once. Prisoners have an incentive not to confess if they intend to commit more crimes together.

But that does not answer the question of what the optimal strategy is to incentivize cooperation from other players when playing an iterated game. Should we take a New Testament approach and always cooperate, regardless of the actions of the other players? Alternatively, should we look to the Old Testament and follow an eye-for-an-eye strategy, punishing those who do not cooperate and never turning the other cheek? Or is the best strategy a mix of the two?

The answer comes from a Soviet refugee who survived the Russian Revolution of 1917 and Lenin's terrors.

And the answer is surprisingly simple.

CHAPTER 3

Iterated Games: Be Nice, Retaliate, and Forgive

Anatol Rapoport: Skating on Thin Ice

Anatol Rapoport (1911–2007) was an American mathematician who made important contributions to the social sciences and biology, authoring more than three hundred papers and two dozen books. He was most famous for the formulation of an optimal strategy for the prisoner's dilemma when the game is played multiple times between the same players. He was also an early and important leader of various peace movements in the United States and Canada. Much of his later life was taken up with research about game theory and war.

Rapoport was the only child of a Jewish couple who lived in Lozova, Russia, an industrial town that today is part of eastern Ukraine.[1] Rapoport was identified early on as a gifted musician and began formal training in classical piano at the age of five. He also evidenced an affinity with languages and in grade school read widely in Russian, English, German, and French. The Russian Revolution of 1917 did not significantly affect his family, but the subsequent civil war was particularly harsh because of food shortages and the growing persecution of Jews. In addition, the Rapoport family lived in a "White" region of Russia that was particularly targeted by the Bolsheviks for opposing the Russian Revolution.

In 1921, Rapoport's parents decided to flee the Soviet Union to live with relatives in Chicago. The family first traveled by train to the Polish border. Rapoport's mother was smuggled out of the country, and days later Anatol was instructed by his father to skate over the frozen Zbruch River to where his mother was waiting on the Polish side. But a Soviet border guard spotted Rapoport and aimed his rifle at the boy. Rapoport quickly scampered back to shore. Several nights later his father was able to bribe a Soviet border guard, and father and son escaped to Poland. The family traveled to France, boarded a ship bound for America, passed through Ellis Island, and then traveled by train to Chicago.

As a boy, Rapoport earned money by teaching piano to other neighborhood children and as an accompanist for theatrical shows. After high school, he went to Vienna, Austria, for five years to study music and graduated with a degree in composition, piano, and conducting from the Academy of Music and the Performing Arts, where his teacher was a "grand-pupil" of Franz Liszt. During this time, he held well-received concerts in Austria, Italy, Hungary, and Poland. However, with the rise of Hitler, the opportunities for a Jewish musician were diminishing in German-speaking Europe, so he returned to America in 1934. Although he held concerts in New York City and Chicago and continued to perform regularly for the rest of his life, Rapoport decided to go back to college, where he discovered mathematics. He entered the University of Chicago as a first-year student in 1937 and graduated with a PhD in mathematics in 1941.

Two days after Rapoport received his doctorate, the Japanese attacked Pearl Harbor. Rapoport immediately enlisted, briefly taught mathematics to Air Force cadets, and then was sent to Alaska as part of America's clandestine operation to supply the Soviet Union with US military aircraft. American pilots would fly C-47s, P-40s, A-20s, and B-25s to Fairbanks, and then Russian pilots would fly the military aircraft across the Bering Strait to the Soviet Union and on to Stalingrad and Voronezh to battle with Hitler's Luftwaffe. Rapoport was soon promoted to captain and served as the supply officer, control tower officer, and interpreter. In his autobiography, Rapoport reports how much he enjoyed the friendships he developed with many Russian military aviators on the secret US military base in Nome, Alaska. He writes that these friendships were "the kind that feeds among Russians on endless conversations, most soul-searching."[2] He also recounts his sadness at the deaths of many of these Russian pilots, flying unfamiliar US aircraft under the cover of darkness in the harsh conditions of the blustery Arctic.[3]

In 1944, Rapoport volunteered for another tour of duty and served as a military supply officer in what is now Dhaka, Bangladesh. His job was to organize the transport of gasoline "over the hump" of the Himalayas in C-54 cargo planes to China.[4] Rapoport once again established friendships with the pilots—though this time they were Chinese instead of Russian. He also attended many of their funerals because the planes laden with gasoline sometimes exploded. Among those killed was Rapoport's roommate.[5] Rapoport returned to academic life in 1947. He taught at the University of Chicago as part of the Committee on Mathematical Biology and published his first academic papers. He also met his wife, Gwen, to whom he proposed in 1948 at 6:00 p.m. on New Year's Eve, after only three dates. (He would continue to celebrate their marriage by repeating that ritual every year on the same date and time until his death fifty-eight years later.)

In 1954, Rapoport was awarded a year's fellowship at the Center for Advanced Study in the Behavioral Sciences on the Stanford University campus. During that year, his focus shifted away from mathematics and biology. He came to oppose the notion of "all science as value-free and therefore morally neutral and merely instrumental."[6] Rapoport became convinced that researchers in the physical, social, and life sciences had to take responsibility for the "goals of any social policy" that science enabled.[7] During the initial phase of the Cold War in the 1950s, this was a radical viewpoint, even among academics.

In 1955, when he returned from Stanford, Rapoport took a position at the University of Michigan with the objective of studying what he called "the three arms of the peace movement: peace research, peace education and peace activism."[8] Rapoport used his background in math and biology to publish multiple books on game theory and international conflict. He also became one of the leading peace activists on American campuses. Beginning in the early 1960s, he vocally opposed the Vietnam War in speeches throughout the country. One of his frequent lines was that the Vietnam War was a "war against humanity" that "we shall not win."[9] Rapoport is credited as one of the leaders of the first teach-in, an alternative to a teachers' strike involving lectures and seminars, which was held at the University of Michigan on the night of March 24–25, 1965. The practice of teach-ins spread to campuses across the country during the late 1960s and early 1970s. (Rapoport also was a leader of a group of scientists who raised money for John Nash's treatment and care during this time.)

By the late 1960s, Rapoport was becoming increasingly frustrated by the unresponsiveness of the American government to protests against the Vietnam War. In 1970, he decided to move to Canada "to live in a country that was not committed to a messianic role" and "with no aspiration to major power status."[10] He accepted a position as a professor of mathematics and psychology at the University of Toronto and remained there until he left in 1980 to become director of the Institute of Advanced Studies in Vienna. He returned to Canada in 1984 to take the newly created position of professor of peace studies, a role he held until he retired in 1996. He also joined a newly formed organization, Science for Peace, that continues to the present day as a forum for scientists to promote a more peaceful world, and served as the organization's president for two years. When once asked if he was a pacifist, Rapoport replied that he preferred to call himself an abolitionist because "I'm for killing the institution of war."[11]

For the last half century of his life, Rapoport was committed to research that fostered greater cooperation among nations. He believed that a better understanding of game theory offered prospects for a more peaceful world.

He wrote in his autobiography near the end of his life:

> *Preoccupation with game theory led me to scrutinize . . . the sharp distinction between individual and collective rationality. . . . The relevance of these findings to the increasingly widely recognized global problems became a constantly recurring theme in my preoccupation and expression.*[12]

The Prisoner's Dilemma:
The Role of Communication

Rapoport's groundbreaking and popular book *Fights, Games, and Debates* was published in 1960 and was addressed to "serious students of human conflict."[13] In this book, Rapoport wrote that "what is essentially missing from game theory proper is a rigorous analysis of situations where communicative acts are moves of the game, and where effective communication may change the game."[14]

In the case of the prisoner's dilemma, Rapoport realized that communicating with the other player fundamentally changed the nature of the game. In testing Nash's theory, the two RAND researchers had effectively communicated the following message: cooperate with me and I will cooperate with you in return. That message was delivered in the form of actions taken by the players in sequential rounds of the game. As Nash had rightly pointed out, if the two RAND researchers had been replaced by another pair of RAND researchers after each round, then cooperation would probably never have developed. Because the two RAND researchers could effectively communicate their intentions to cooperate if the other reciprocated in kind, this changed the optimal strategy for both players.

Rapoport broke down conflicts into three types, which make up the title of his book. In "fights," at least one side communicates that they will never cooperate. Given that one side will never cooperate, the only rational decision is for the other side to do the same. In "games," players reward cooperation and punish competition during the game. In "debates," players try to persuade others to cooperate outside of actions taken in the game. For example, players may talk before the game starts and encourage others to cooperate.

Rapoport realized that once communication becomes an important part of game theory, the discipline moves beyond mathematics. To determine an optimal strategy, players must make subjective judgments about the intentions of the others and then determine whether others are attempting to deceive them. Rapoport understood that in real-life games these subjective judgments could be more important in determining outcomes than the deductions that flow from the axioms of game theory.

Hence, Rapoport shifted the focus of his research on game theory from pure mathematics to behavioral science.

No More Superhumans: From Theory to Practice

This shift is obvious in the chapter on the prisoner's dilemma in *Fights, Games, and Debates*. After introducing the concept behind the prisoner's dilemma, Rapoport immediately delves into an experiment conducted by Morton Deutsch at Bell Labs in which individuals were asked to play a version of the prisoner's dilemma. The results of the experiment showed that communication increased the overall level of cooperation. Among participants who were prevented from communicating with each other, only 12 percent cooperated.[15] By comparison, the rate of cooperation was 58 percent for those who were allowed to speak with each other before the game.[16] Rapoport argued that game theory depends to a large extent on the beliefs of the players about the intentions of other players, and therefore the limits of human rationality become a critical factor.

Rapoport correctly pointed out that humans are not machines able to coldly calculate payoffs and unerringly deduce optimal strategies. Among the examples he provided is one drawn from his experience during World War II in military aviation. It relates to a proposal an officer once made to save the lives of military airmen.

Rapoport wrote:

> *In World War II at a certain bomber base in the South Pacific a flier's chances of surviving his quota of thirty missions were rated at 25 percent. The young men lived the life of the doomed. Then a way was found to improve the situation.*[17]

The "way" was a proposal to increase bomb payloads to reduce the number of required missions. However, increasing payloads would necessitate cutting back on fuel in order for the planes to get airborne, which meant some of the planes would not make it safely back to base. Rapoport noted that this proposal was rejected out of hand by military leaders and by the airmen themselves. Although the proposal would have likely saved lives, it did not take into account the human element. The idea that some crews were doomed from the start was unacceptable for most. Rapoport showed that the rational choice may be rejected even by those whose lives depend on it. Rapoport also gave a hypothetical example of a mother whose two sons are held as hostages. The mother is told that if she selects one son to be shot, the other will be spared. If she refuses to decide which of her sons will die, then both will be killed. The rational decision is to name a son to be killed. But Rapoport rightly observed that "under these conditions many a mother would refuse to make the choice."[18] The rational choice about one's flesh and blood is a choice that many people are often unable to make.

Hence, Rapoport argued that game theory should rely on experiments with real people to make predictions about the outcomes of conflicts, rather than relying solely on deductions from mathematical axioms that assume perfect rationality.

He wrote:

> *We are thus led away from a "static" conception of game theory, namely a rationality based on a complete knowledge of an existing state of affairs coupled with superhuman powers of deduction. We become aware of . . . acting on hypotheses, to affect the environment, in particular perceptions of other actors.*[19]

In his 1965 book, *Prisoner's Dilemma*, coauthored with Albert Chammah, Rapoport wrote about the results from an experiment he conducted at the University of Michigan, the first of its kind to scientifically test the willingness of individuals to cooperate when confronted by the prisoner's dilemma.

Experimenting on Undergraduates (and Untrusting Women)

The experiment Rapoport wrote about in *Prisoner's Dilemma* involved hundreds of pairs of undergraduates who played the prisoner's dilemma three hundred times in succession.[20] At that time, game theorists typically labeled the players' responses in the prisoner's dilemma as either cooperating or confessing. But Rapoport found that confusing, as both terms started with a C, and so he referred to confessing as "defection," which has become the nomenclature adopted by game theorists to the present day.[21]

The data showed that, at first, individuals were almost evenly split on whether to cooperate or defect. Many of those who experienced defection in response to cooperation in the first round then punished defection by responding in kind, and thus cooperation quickly declined. However, after thirty rounds, most of the players had communicated with their opponent through their actions that defection would be punished. In response to punishment, the defecting player learned it was better to cooperate. Levels of cooperation reached 55 percent after 100 rounds and 70 percent by 150 rounds and continued to climb steadily thereafter. By halfway through the experiment, a consistent pattern had emerged: most pairs consistently cooperated, although a minority were locked into rounds of repeated retaliatory, punishing defections.[22]

Rapoport also found "striking differences" in how men and women responded.[23] Both sexes began the game with similar degrees of cooperation. However, as the game progressed, marked disparities emerged in how men and women reacted to one another. When men played against men or women, there was a similar willingness to cooperate. But women playing against women were much more likely to retaliate against defection and unlikely to repay cooperation with cooperation. In addition, when playing against each other, women frequently spiraled into rounds of sustained defection. When playing against men, women were "pulled up toward men's levels of cooperation" and men were "slightly pulled down."[24] In short, women showed significantly less willingness to trust other women and were slightly less trusting in general.

For Rapoport, these experiments carried more weight than mathematical theory. As he wrote in *Prisoner's Dilemma*:

> *People choose on various occasions the one or the other alternative and their choices can be represented as frequencies, including several degrees of contingency, which perhaps depend on certain conditions. Thus, one proceeds to construct a theory solely from the statistical regularities one observes in the data. . . . Attempts to analyze it carry one deeper and deeper into a maze*

of intricate and interrelated questions, which are impossible to keep on a purely "rational," i.e., strategy-calculating level.[25]

Rapoport also believed it was important to apply the lessons learned from game theory to the real world, given the potential for nuclear war to end life on Earth as we know it. Rapoport explained in one of his unpublished manuscripts:

> *The present dangerous situation has arisen because there is a lack of "trust" among nations. . . . The prisoner's dilemma provides a simple but dramatic demonstration of the sort of thinking that must be changed in the nuclear age. . . . This manner of thinking now threatens the human race with extinction.*[26]

In addition to behavioral experiments, Rapoport suggested that insights could be gained from games played with computers. In his book *Strategy and Conscience*, Rapoport talks about "computers as simulators . . . and from the results so obtained one can see how a real system would behave if it were characterized by the values assigned to its parameters."[27]

However, at the time Rapoport wrote the *Prisoner's Dilemma*, machines did not yet have the computing power to simulate more than the most simplistic models of game theory and the prisoner's dilemma. But that would all change during the 1980s.

The War between the Machines: The Tit-for-Tat Terminator

As an undergraduate at the University of Chicago during the 1960s, Robert Axelrod studied mathematics and became familiar with Rapoport's work. He went on to get a PhD in political science at

Yale University in 1969 and taught at Berkeley until 1974, when he accepted a professorship at the University of Michigan. Axelrod's professional career would follow Rapoport's not just geographically but also intellectually. As Axelrod reported in an interview years later, "I didn't know Anatol Rapoport personally . . . [but] I owe him a great debt."[28]

Axelrod had read *Fights, Games, and Debates* as an undergraduate and then *Prisoner's Dilemma* as a graduate student and became fascinated by game theory. Like Rapoport, Axelrod believed the lessons from game theory could help humanity avoid the catastrophe of nuclear war. Unlike Rapoport, Axelrod thought "trying to analyze how humans play the game would not be sufficient, because humans tend to become bored and will try almost anything now and then."[29] Instead, Axelrod decided to "conduct tournaments for the iterated Prisoner's Dilemma based on submissions from people who understand the game."[30]

In 1980, Axelrod invited professional game theorists from five disciplines—psychology, economics, political science, mathematics, and sociology—to submit computer programs that would play a version of the prisoner's dilemma against each other in a round-robin tournament.[31] Fourteen individuals responded with programs that varied in length from four to seventy-seven internal steps. Each game consisted of two hundred rounds to give the programs sufficient time to interact with each other and allow for the emergence of cooperation.

Because the competition involved computer programs, Axelrod created a simple payoff matrix to represent the prisoner's dilemma: cooperation by both programs resulted in an award of 3 points, whereas defection by both yielded only 1 point. If one program defected and the other cooperated, then the defecting program was rewarded with 5 points and the cooperating program received no points. In terms of the prisoner's dilemma, the points can be thought of as a reduction in the length of a prison sentence. If both prisoners refuse to confess, then the length of the sentence is reduced by three years, but if both confess, the sentence is reduced by only one year. If one prisoner confesses and the other does not, then the prisoner who confesses earns a five-year reduction in sentence. Thus, the optimal strategy is to confess, regardless of what the other prisoner does, if the game is played only once.

Unfortunately for the prisoners, both will reason similarly, and so both will confess, which will result in a reduction in prison time of only one year. If the two prisoners had cooperated and not confessed, then three years would have been knocked off their respective sentences. When each prisoner follows their own self-interest, they both end up serving more jail time.

In Axelrod's tournament, every program competed once with every other program, once with itself, and once with a program Axelrod created called Random, which behaved exactly as its name implies, randomly cooperating and defecting. Given two hundred rounds, the best score a program could achieve would be 1,000 points (5×200), in the case of always defecting against a program that naïvely always cooperated. The worst score would be 0 (0×200), for a clueless program that always cooperated in response to defection. If two programs always cooperated with each other (or themselves), they would earn 600 points (3×200).

The program that won was submitted by Anatol Rapoport. Rapoport called his program Tit-for-Tat (TFT). It was the program with the least number of internal steps (four) and contained the simplest set of rules of all the programs. TFT started with a cooperative move and then responded with what the other program did on the previous move. By contrast, some of the programs were exceptionally complicated: Look Ahead employed artificial intelligence, and Downing used conditional probability and advanced statistical techniques to inform its decisions. Other programs were variations on TFT. Joss began with a cooperative move and then followed what the other player did on the previous move, except that 10 percent of the time, it would randomly defect in response to cooperation to sneak in a few more points. Another program, labeled Friedman, started with a cooperative move but would respond to a defection by defecting the balance of the game, severely punishing a program that failed to cooperate even once.

Tit-for-Tat: Nice, Retaliatory, Forgiving, and Clear

After the tournament, Axelrod analyzed the outcomes and determined that four characteristics were responsible for the success of TFT against the other programs.

The first was that TFT was "nice," defined as never the first to defect. In fact, being nice was the most important determiner of success in the tournament: the eight highest-ranking programs were all nice, and the bottom seven (the other six programs submitted plus Random) were not. The importance of this characteristic can be seen by comparing TFT with a hypothetical "not nice" program, Always Defect. In a head-to-head competition between TFT and Always Defect, the latter will always win. That is because TFT begins with cooperation, which Always Defect responds to with defection, earning 5 points. Then TFT and Always Defect punish each other for the remaining 199 moves, and each is awarded 1 point per move. Thus, when TFT and Always Defect are paired, Always Defect outscores TFT by 5 points. However, when paired with itself, TFT more than compensates for this loss by cooperating for all two hundred moves and racking up 600 points by earning 3 points per move. By contrast, Always Defect paired with itself earns only 200 points, defecting every time. As the nicest of all programs submitted, TFT suffered narrow losses head-to-head against every other program, including Random. But this small loss was more than offset by a large gain when playing against itself compared with the other less nice programs. The less nice programs all experienced significantly lower rates of cooperation than TFT when competing against themselves.

The second important characteristic is that TFT is "retaliatory." Suppose TFT was competing with a hypothetical nice program called Always Cooperate. When TFT and Always Cooperate compete and play against themselves, both programs score 600 points (3 × 200). However, Always Cooperate does significantly worse against Random, earning no points whenever Random defects. All programs submitted were to some extent retaliatory, and the lack of this characteristic is why Random finished last.

The third characteristic is that TFT is "forgiving" after the initial punishment. Imagine TFT was competing with Friedman, which responds to a single defection with an unending stream of defections. Head-to-head, TFT and Friedman will cooperate, and when playing against themselves, they will earn 600 points (3 × 200). However, Friedman will forever punish Random after the first defection and thereafter will never benefit from the higher points earned through cooperation.

The fourth characteristic is that TFT is "clear." The response of TFT to either cooperation or defection is easily discernible by the other programs. Suppose TFT was competing with Joss, which randomly defects 10 percent of the time. Joss will defeat TFT head-to-head because Joss will periodically earn 5 points when TFT responds to cooperation in kind and Joss defects. However, when Joss plays against itself, random defections will trigger a downward spiral of defections. Similarly, when Joss plays against other programs, they will interpret a random defection by Joss as a sign that it is punishing them for no apparent reason, and therefore will be less willing to cooperate. On the other hand, TFT makes clear its intentions: it will consistently respond in kind.

Axelrod summarized his findings as follows:

What accounts for TIT-FOR-TAT's robust success is its combination of being nice, retaliatory, forgiving and clear. Its niceness prevents it from getting into unnecessary trouble. Its retaliation discourages the other side from persisting whenever defection is tried. Its forgiveness helps restore mutual cooperation. And its clarity makes it intelligible to the other players, thereby eliciting long-term cooperation.[32]

Axelrod analyzed the data and saw that the programs that were unable to cooperate with others (and themselves) suffered from lower average scores than TFT when playing similarly uncooperative programs. Conversely, TFT enjoyed higher average scores when encountering more cooperative programs like itself. So Axelrod concluded that the "effectiveness of a particular strategy depends not on its own characteristics, but also on the nature of the other strategies with which it must interact."[33]

For this reason, Axelrod decided to conduct a second tournament.

In the second tournament, all entrants were given a detailed analysis of the outcomes from the first. This time, a total of sixty-two entries were received from six countries. The contestants ranged from a ten-year-old computer hobbyist to game theorists from eight different disciplines of academia. Many of the entrants created programs specifically devised to defeat TFT, given the success of the program in the first tournament. Although the rules allowed the submission of any program, including any of those written by others in the first tournament, only one entrant submitted TFT.

That entrant was Anatol Rapoport. And he won again.

The contestants in the second tournament had learned some lessons from the first. Most programs were nice, and nearly all were forgiving. But when speaking with the entrants, Axelrod learned that some players had anticipated that others would conclude that being nice and forgiving was the best strategy, and therefore the number of programs sharing these characteristics would be larger than in the first tournament. Hence, some entrants intentionally developed programs to take advantage of what they expected to be a large population of nice and forgiving programs. But in the end, the programs that were not nice or forgiving dragged down their scores through sustained rounds of defection when they encountered each other and themselves.

Nevertheless, Axelrod suspected that TFT might not win every contest and that its success was partly based on the characteristics of the other programs. Thus, he created six new tournaments using the programs submitted for the second tournament and varied portions of each program type. TFT still won five of the six tournaments. (TFT barely lost the one tournament against a slightly different version of itself.) This clearly demonstrated that a winning strategy partly depends on the nature of the opponents. But it also showed the robustness of TFT in a variety of environments.

In the above examples, we have seen how there is an incentive to cooperate if cooperation will be rewarded and not to defect if defection will be punished.[34] Axelrod's tournament demonstrated that Rapoport's TFT was the best strategy in the simple world of battling computer programs.

But payoffs frequently cannot be expressed with the same quantitative precision outside of computer tournaments, and choices are rarely as binary as cooperate or defect. Yet, in the real world, there are many examples of TFT.

Trench Warfare: He Ain't a Bad Fellow

During World War I, an example of TFT developed in the trenches between soldiers of the Allied and Central powers.[35]

In the early twentieth century, the basic unit of warfare was a battalion, about one thousand men. When World War I began, it was exceptionally bloody, as Allied battalions confronted Central powers forces of similar size across several hundred yards of no-man's-land. However, as the lines stabilized and opposing battalions regularly engaged each other, a pattern of nonaggression emerged without the benefit of direct communication between enemy forces.

An eyewitness at the front lines reported, "In one section the hour of 8 to 9 a.m. was regarded as consecrated to private business and certain places indicated by a flag were regarded as out of bounds by the snipers on both sides."[36]

A soldier wrote in his diary: "We go out at night in front of the trenches. . . . The German working parties are also out, so it is not considered etiquette to fire."[37]

A similar pattern of nonaggression also emerged to enable deliveries of fresh rations. Artillery fire was often directed away from supply lines.

As an artillery officer related:

> *It would be child's play to shell the road behind the enemy's trenches, crowded with ration wagons . . . [but] if you prevent your enemy from drawing his rations, his remedy is simple: he will prevent you from drawing yours.*[38]

This pattern of nonaggression was directly at odds with the objectives of those back at army headquarters. The generals were playing an extended game of attrition in which the greater the number of enemy casualties, the better. (See Chapter 6 for more on the game theory of wars of attrition.) By contrast, the soldiers down in the trenches were playing a life-or-death daily game of the prisoner's dilemma. So commanders at army headquarters had to develop a way to break the patterns of nonaggression that emerged between opposing battalions confronting each other across the battlefields of Europe.

The first approach used to combat these unwelcome outbreaks of peace was to rotate battalions on a weekly basis. The goal of these rotations was to destroy whatever previous patterns of cooperation had emerged. However, a practice arose of the outgoing unit informing the incoming unit of the tacit understandings that had been reached, allowing the established patterns of cooperation to continue. One English soldier advised his replacement, "Mr. Bosche ain't a bad fellow. You leave 'im alone; he'll leave you alone."[39]

In the end, national military commanders resorted to ordering periodic raids to compel soldiers to fight. By forcing soldiers to "go over the top," unspoken nonaggression pacts between opposing enemy battalions were broken. Launching a raid, the equivalent of defecting, triggered a response in kind by the other side in the form of a retaliatory raid, and spiraling rounds of defections would ensue.

During World War I, military commanders, whether consciously or not, ensured that the deadly game of prisoner's dilemma that played out in the trenches was marked by ruinous rounds of defections, leading to the deaths of millions of soldiers.

International Trade Agreements: The Exception Is the Rule

Trade wars are the economic equivalent of the prisoner's dilemma with spiraling rounds of defection. Nation A slaps tariffs on the goods of Nation B to improve its terms of trade, and Nation B retaliates with tariffs on the goods of Nation A. In the end, both nations are worse off, as the flow of goods between the nations is reduced and neither country is able to establish more favorable terms of trade. On the other hand, treaties that reduce trade barriers between nations are the equivalent of sustained rounds of cooperation. Through cutting or eliminating tariffs, nations benefit from the economic gains of comparative advantage by doing what they do best and trading for the rest. In the TFT of international trade policy, nations reward other countries that allow foreign companies greater access to their domestic markets, and punish those who do not.

Unfortunately, the current international trade regime exhibits a particular kind of prisoner's dilemma that encourages defection in the form of free trade agreements (FTAs).[40] Most international trade is currently governed by the World Trade Organization (WTO). The primary tools the WTO uses to combat trade barriers are most favored nation (MFN) agreements. These agreements stipulate that a WTO member cannot grant selective access to its domestic markets, most commonly in the form of lower tariffs. If a WTO member "defects" by raising tariffs on one member, then it must subject all members to the same tariff. But this defection also invites a retaliatory response by all 150 current members of the WTO. Hence, there is an incentive for each WTO member nation to keep trade barriers low.

However, the WTO agreement grants an exception in Article XXIV. This exception allows nations to enter into an FTA, and that exception has become the rule. The European Union provides MFN treatment to nine WTO members. But the European Union has FTAs with 153 other WTO members that are more favorable than MFN rates.[41] In total, more than four hundred FTAs have been put in place since the formation of the WTO.[42]

In terms of the prisoner's dilemma, implementing trade policy through the WTO with MFNs is the equivalent of cooperating. Pursuing bilateral trade deals by FTAs is a form of defection. An individual nation can have the best of both worlds as a member of the WTO by taking advantage of an MFN with all nations while benefiting from FTAs with a selected group of countries. As one study concluded, "Each country [within the WTO] does even better when it unilaterally exploits the terms of trade consequences of its policy choices and thereby redistributes surplus from its trading partner to itself."[43]

If nations continue to act in their own self-interest by establishing FTAs, then eventually all nations will suffer from the collapse of the WTO and the loss of MFN agreements.

Corporate Warfare: Repeat Customers and Employees

Businesspeople frequently agree to exchange goods and services without detailed and extensive legal contracts. A survey of a large manufacturer of packing materials revealed that over a four-year period, more than half of all transactions had no agreement on the specific terms and conditions of the sale or any legal agreement in place at all.[44] Even when legal contracts exist, few businesses are willing to litigate but instead settle disputes outside of the courts. One analysis showed that in a typical year less than 3 percent of civil suits filed in US district courts involved commercial contracts.[45] The same analysis showed that many purchasing agents had never been involved in a dispute that had gone to court.[46] As a purchasing agent explained, "You don't read legalistic contract clauses at each other if you ever want to do business again. One doesn't run to the lawyers if he wants to stay in business."[47]

Resorting to the legal system to resolve conflicts is the equivalent of mutual defection in the prisoner's dilemma: both sides are worse off because of delays and legal fees. Agreeing to settle a commercial dispute outside the legal system is a form of cooperation that saves time and money. And the more frequently the two sides deal with each other, the more incentive for buyers and sellers to cooperate. There is a greater temptation for the seller to cheat a one-time buyer than a repeat customer, just as in the prisoner's dilemma, there is no incentive to cooperate if the game is played only once.

The benefits of being a repeat customer extend not only between but also within businesses. Large corporations depend on extensive bureaucracies to function—with all the associated inefficiencies. However, there is one clear benefit to big business: establishing layers of trust between the company and its employees.

In theory, there is no reason for the existence of a large corporation. A company could comprise a small group of purchasing managers who could contract with individual workers to supply their labor in return for wages. A 100 percent outsourced firm would have the flexibility to contract with any laborer in the economy, enabling the company to find the most efficient and productive worker for a particular task. In contrast, a large corporation assigns tasks to in-house employees, who are unlikely to be the best person in the nation for a given job. In addition, a 100 percent outsourced firm would have more leverage over its workers, forcing independent contractors to compete on price and service. At a large corporation, firing an employee for a job not done well has much higher frictional costs than terminating a gig worker.

However, a large corporation benefits from workers who deal regularly with the company and each other. Workers within a large company are playing multiple rounds of a version of the prisoner's dilemma and have an incentive to cooperate by not cheating their employer or fellow workers. In comparison, a hypothetical outsourced firm may deal with a particular worker infrequently, and that worker may infrequently interact with other workers hired by that company. Workers contracted by an outsourced firm may be playing a version of the prisoner's dilemma that has only one or a few rounds and the associated incentives for defection.

In my view, an important reason for the success of large corporations is that employees have an incentive to cooperate when interacting with the company and each other. Big business works partly because employees are repeat suppliers.

Baseball: Good Nights and Bad Days

Another example of TFT comes from baseball.[48] Ron Luciano, a baseball umpire, related in his memoirs that he occasionally had "bad days." He defined bad days as those that followed "good nights." On one of his bad days, he would let the catcher umpire for him. If the pitch was a strike, then the catcher was instructed to hold his glove in place for an extra second. If the pitch was a ball, then the catcher would throw the ball right back. Luciano claimed that "no one I worked with ever took advantage of the situation, and no hitter ever figured out what I was doing."[49]

Luciano was able to successfully outsource his job on bad days and keep this arrangement quiet because the catcher knew the umpire would punish him on future good days if he did not cooperate.

Conclusions

We have seen how cooperation can emerge in an iterated game of the prisoner's dilemma. Based on the success of TFT in Axelrod's tournaments, we can make four general conclusions about how to avoid being outplayed by others and how to achieve greater levels of cooperation:

1. *Be nice.* The best predictor of success in Axelrod's tournament was whether a program was the first to defect. An initial defection will likely set off retaliation by the other

player. But if you cooperate from the start, then you can hopefully establish a pattern of cooperation that will continue. And you will have also discovered the willingness of the other player to cooperate.

2. *Retaliate.* Axelrod demonstrated that an-eye-for-an-eye justice was more effective in fostering cooperation. TFT never turns the other cheek: an-eye-for-an-eye is a better way to ensure cooperation than the Golden Rule.

3. *Forgive afterward.* TFT punished defection only once. Other programs, such as Friedman, which punished defection for the rest of the game, were caught in spiraling rounds of defection, unable to cooperate most of the time. Do not let your opponent play you, but give them an incentive to cooperate by forgiving after retaliating.

4. *Be clear.* Part of the success of TFT was that its strategy was easily understood by the other players. Other players are trying to adapt their strategies to yours to find out whether there is a way to cooperate with you. If the other players do not understand your strategy, then they have no way to do this. If you are clear about the second point above, then they cannot use this knowledge to take advantage of you.

We have seen that in most situations the best strategy is TFT. However, TFT does not always win. Recall that in one of Axelrod's subsequent tournaments, TFT lost to a program that used a similar strategy. This was because the composition of the other programs in that tournament differed from the composition of the programs in the previous tournaments. So the success of a particular strategy will partly depend on the strategies followed by others.

One of the first to understand this was a biologist who would extend the idea of TFT beyond the confines of mathematics and behavioral science into the natural world. He also realized there were parallels between game theory and evolution. This biologist discovered that animals, insects, and plants played out their own version of TFT in the literal dog-eat-dog world of natural selection, where the strategies adopted by others mean the difference between life and death.

He was also inclined to believe that each individual acting in their own self-interest would leave society collectively worse off. This belief was consistent with his membership in the Communist Party of Great Britain.

CHAPTER 4

Evolution:
Males Are the Problem

John Maynard Smith: Sex Scientist

John Maynard Smith (1920–2004), widely known in academic circles as JMS, was a mathematical biologist and geneticist who developed, with George Price, the theory of an evolutionarily stable strategy (ESS). Trained in engineering and zoology, JMS published more than a hundred academic papers and wrote a series of books on evolutionary biology. During his career JMS received many honors, including election as a Fellow of the Royal Society and the Darwin, Royal, and Copley medals.

JMS was the son of an upper-class Edinburgh mother and a London surgeon who died when JMS was just eight years old. The future co-discoverer of ESS had a passion as a child for studying insects and animals. He was educated at Eton, although he disliked many of his classmates and found them "snobbish and anti-intellectual."[1] At fourteen, he became an atheist after reading Darwin.

In 1938, JMS traveled to Berlin to visit his uncle, who was the British military attaché. His uncle had become virulently anti-Nazi during his posting in Germany and went as far as to hatch a plot to assassinate Hitler using a sniper posted on the roof of the French embassy.[2] The British government got word of the scheme and squashed it. Based on what JMS witnessed in Nazi Germany, he came back to England vehemently anti-fascist. At that time, the Communist Party of Great Britain was the most anti-Nazi political organization in the United Kingdom, so JMS joined up while a student at Cambridge.

When war broke out, he volunteered but, because of poor eyesight, was told to return to university. JMS said his poor eyesight was an evolutionary advantage because "it stopped me getting shot."[3] He graduated in 1941 and initially went to work designing military aircraft. But after the war ended, he quit his job as an aeronautical engineer to study zoology at the graduate school of the University College London (UCL). Although he never earned a doctorate, his brilliance led to an appointment as a lecturer at UCL, where one of his students was a young Alan Turing.[4]

In 1956, the Soviets invaded Hungary, and JMS quit the Communist Party of Great Britain. He was still committed to many of the ideals of Marxism but was disillusioned by Stalin. In 1965, JMS left UCL to become the founding dean of the School of Biological Sciences at the University of Sussex. He retired in 1985 but continued to publish papers and write books until his death in 2004.

Richard Dawkins, a leading evolutionary biologist, said of JMS:

There is scarcely a branch of evolutionary or population genetic theory that has not been illuminated

by his vivid and versatile inventiveness. . . . He is
one of the rare company of scientists that changes
the way people think.[5]

JMS had a broad impact on our views concerning evolution and the behavior of animals. And he changed how we think about sex.

Hawks and Doves

In his book *Evolution and the Theory of Games*, JMS put forward the theory of an ESS. The basic idea was that "ESS is a strategy such that, if all the members of a population adopt it, then no mutant strategy could invade the population under the influence of natural selection."[6] JMS believed this theory had wide application from "the growth form of a plant, or the age at first reproduction, or the relative numbers of sons and daughters produced by a parent."[7] He was also convinced that his theory extended beyond biology to include how natural selection shaped animal and human behavior.

Unlike the examples of TFT in the previous chapter, JMS did not think that these behaviors are the product of willful intention. Lions did not consciously decide one day not to cooperate with gazelles. Rather, lions that fail to cooperate with gazelles feed more often, live longer, and have more cubs.[8] Lions that display a similar approach to other lions do not. JMS understood that animal behavior was not the product of deliberate, conscious signaling, like two humans playing an iterated prisoner's game. Instead, these behaviors emerge from an ESS between competing organisms.

As an example, JMS cites an experiment involving two pigs in a large pen.[9] The pigs fed themselves by pressing a lever that caused food to be dispensed at the far side of the pen away from the lever. A stable pattern of behavior developed between the two pigs: the dominant pig would press the lever while the subordinate pig waited in front of the food dispenser and ate until the dominant pig arrived to push the subordinate pig away. This is the only possible ESS. If the subordinate pig presses the lever, then the dominant pig prevents the subordinate pig from eating, and eventually the subordinate pig will stop pressing the lever. This pattern of behavior will continue even when the amount of food dispensed is reduced to the point that the subordinate pig eats most of the food before the dominant pig reaches the other side of the pen.[10] The two pigs did not negotiate this arrangement: an ESS was established because it was the only sustainable pattern of behavior.

To illustrate how these types of behaviors can emerge, JMS created the example of a game of "hawks" and "doves."[11] The game revolves around two animals competing for a piece of food lying on a rock. When two hawks meet, they fight until one is seriously injured, and the victorious bird gets the food. When two doves meet, they divide up the food equally. When a hawk confronts a dove, the dove flies away, and the hawk gets the food. In evolutionary terms, greater amounts of food and fewer instances of serious injury result in more hatchlings. Over time, either hawks or doves, depending on which gains more food and suffers fewer injuries, will come to dominate the population through natural selection. The question JMS sought to answer is whether playing hawk or dove is an ESS.

Note there are parallels between the hawk-dove game and Axelrod's tournament from the previous chapter.

The hawk strategy can be thought of as the equivalent of defection. When two hawks meet, one will get the food, but both will be seriously injured. The net outcome for the two hawks after an encounter is the benefit to the winner of the food minus the harm to both birds from injuries. The dove strategy can be considered the same as cooperation. When two doves meet, they agree not to fight, split the food, and avoid damaging each other. Since neither suffers injuries, the combined benefit when two doves meet is greater than the combined benefit gained when two hawks meet, since in the latter case both hawks are injured. Just like in the prisoner's dilemma when criminals cooperate, the net gain to the two birds in total is greater by the adoption of a dove strategy.

In the case of Axelrod's tournament, we saw how the composition of the other programs in the contest impacts the success of a particular strategy. A program such as Always Cooperate will lose if all the other programs in the contest are Always Defect. But Always Cooperate does just as well as TFT if those are the only two programs in the contest. Similarly, the success of a particular strategy in the hawk-dove game depends on the composition of the initial population of birds. A population of all hawks could not be invaded by a single dove because the sole dove would never be able to acquire a piece of food. However, if a sufficient number of doves invaded a population of hawks, then the doves will share food with each other and survive as a minority within a population that is mostly hawks. By contrast, a sole hawk could invade a population of all doves, as the sole hawk would gain a piece of food after every encounter with a dove.

As we have seen, TFT is the best strategy in Axelrod's tournament when there is some diversification among the other programs. If there was only one TFT program swimming in a sea of Always Defect programs, then TFT would lose the first round and tie the following rounds, leading to a loss of the game overall. However, as long as there is some critical mass of other TFT, Always Cooperate, or other "nice" programs, TFT will eventually win by scoring more points through reciprocal cooperation.

JMS had read Rapoport's books and knew of Axelrod's tournament. He wondered whether TFT in a hawk-dove game was the optimal strategy. In other words, play dove unless the other bird plays hawk, in which case play hawk the next time.

In fact, after the initial two tournaments, Axelrod ran another series of tournaments, one of which simulated TFT in an evolutionary environment. Recall that in Axelrod's first two tournaments the types of programs did not vary over time. But Axelrod recognized that in the case of evolution the winner is rewarded with a greater opportunity to reproduce or, in terms of his tournament, a greater number of copies of a given program in successive rounds. So Axelrod ran another tournament in which "the number of copies (or offspring) of a given entry were proportional to that entry's tournament score."[12] Axelrod believed this "process simulates survival of the fittest."[13] Axelrod conducted his tournament once again, except this time the program with the greatest number of copies running at the end of the contest was declared the winner.

The victory went to TFT.[14]

Given the results of this tournament, JMS suspected that TFT was the optimal strategy in a hawk-dove game. He reasoned that if TFT was the optimal strategy in his hypothetical hawk-dove game, then there would be widespread evidence of TFT behavior in the real world of animals. If TFT was shown empirically to be the dominant strategy among most species, then this would be confirmation that TFT was an ESS.

Over the years, JMS did find instances of TFT in the biological world. One example was an experiment with sticklebacks, a carnivorous freshwater fish.[15] When a larger predatory fish approaches a swarm of sticklebacks, several sticklebacks will swim out to scout the danger to the rest of the school. These scouts take on great personal risk: sometimes a large predatory fish will decide to eat one while the other members of the scouting party bravely flee to warn the others. Given this dynamic, there may be a tendency for each member of the scouting party to hang back a little so as not to be sacrificial sushi. As a result, scouting parties of sticklebacks will move forward in small spurts, then pause and wait to see whether other members of the scouting party have also moved forward. Only after all have moved will one of the sticklebacks again inch toward the waiting jaws of a larger predatory fish. This simple example illustrates TFT in the real life-and-death world of sticklebacks: cooperation in the form of swimming toward danger has to be reciprocated.

However, examples of TFT, such as with the sticklebacks, were not as widespread in the biological world as JMS expected. He realized that the biological world was a lot more complicated than Axelrod's computer tournament.

JMS discovered four key differences.

Computer Programs Do Not Have Relatives

Many species live in groups that are geographically constrained. Therefore, it is likely that in many cases an opponent in a hawk-dove game is related to you. Assuming that natural selection works primarily at the level of genes, then there will be pressure to play dove in order not to injure or kill those spreading your chromosomes. This is particularly true since it is difficult to know beyond the immediate family in the fish or animal world who is a blood relative.

Hence, the genetic factor in biological evolution alters behavior between organisms in a way that a contest between computer programs does not. In Axelrod's tournament, the decision on whether to cooperate or defect depended on the actions of the other player. In the fish and animal world, an opponent could be family, so there is a greater incentive to play dove. As JMS wrote, a person may be "prepared to lay down his life for two brothers or eight cousins."[16]

Computer Programs Value Points the Same

In Axelrod's tournament, the payoffs for cooperation and defection were symmetrical. Similarly, in the prisoner's dilemma, both prisoners reduced their sentences by the same amount by cooperating and added an equal number of years to their prison time by defecting. However, animals and humans regularly experience asymmetrical payoffs when playing a game of hawk-dove.

Several studies have shown that male apes are less likely to be threatened if they are carrying an infant.[17] It is to be expected that a father would fight to protect his child. A father ape has a lot more to lose than the other ape: Dad is fighting to protect his son or daughter, but the attacker is simply looking for a chance to kill an unrelated child. As a result, male apes have developed the habit of carrying around infants that are not their own to reduce the chances of being attacked.[18] The transporting of another ape's progeny is an example of exploiting an opponent's respect for asymmetrical payoffs. Other studies of male apes have also demonstrated that the willingness to fight back when attacked increases with age.[19] This is because an older animal has less to lose than a younger animal, in terms of reproductive years. The asymmetry in payoffs among apes of different ages is consistent with the pattern observed in the wild that older male apes are more likely to play hawk and younger male apes are more likely to play dove.

For many animals, there is a greater benefit to defending their home turf than invading that of another. An animal may have acquired valuable local knowledge, such as where the most watering holes and the least predators are. For the defender, the loss of its home territory can exceed the gain enjoyed by the invader. One example of this was another experiment with stickleback fish (which are, for reasons unknown, a favorite experimental subject with biologists).[20] Two males, male A and male B, built nests at opposite ends of a tank. The two fish were then put into two adjoining glass tubes and were observed trying to attack each other, repeatedly charging the sides of the tubes in an attempt to injure the other fish. Subsequently, the two glass tubes were moved next to the nest of male A. At that point, male A continued to attack while male B retreated. Similarly, when the two glass tubes were relocated next to the nest of male B, he was the aggressor and male A swam away.

A more common example of an asymmetrical payoff that does not involve predatory fish is an encounter between an animal that is fully sated and an animal on the edge of starvation. An animal that needs immediate nourishment to survive will have a greater payoff from gaining access to food. Hence, the hungrier animal has a greater incentive to play hawk. But it can be challenging for two animals fighting over a piece of food to determine who ate last. As a result, an animal may engage in a battle in which the risk of injury exceeds the expected value of the calories gained because it misjudges the level of desperation in its opponent. When the payoff to the opposing player is unknown, it is difficult to know how long and hard to fight.

Computer Programs Do Not Die

In our example of the prisoner's dilemma, the penalty paid by both parties from mutual defection is about the same magnitude as the gain from cooperation. This was also the case in Axelrod's first two tournaments. However, in the animal kingdom, defection can be fatal.

Suppose that in the hawk-dove game, the cost of playing the hawk against another hawk and losing is not serious injury but death. Those who regularly play hawk will be deleted from the gene pool at a higher rate than those who consistently play dove. An analogous situation in Axelrod's tournament would be a rule that one of the defecting programs in cases where both sides defect is eliminated from the tournament. Not many of the programs that regularly defect would survive more than a few rounds.

For this reason, lions prefer to hunt gazelles rather than other lions.[21] When a lion attacks another lion, the defending lion regularly plays hawk, and the nourishment gained is at the potential cost of serious injury or death. When a lion attacks a gazelle, the gazelle plays dove and attempts to run away. If successful, the lion acquires calories from the gazelle at the expense of the calories expended to chase down its prey. Lions feeding on gazelles is an ESS, whereas lions feeding on lions is not. Hence, cannibalism is the exception and not the rule in the animal kingdom.

One strategy guaranteed to work in a hawk-dove game—but only if it's adopted by all members of a community—is to pick fights you expect to lose. This is counterintuitive, which is why it has been referred to as a paradoxical strategy.[22]

To illustrate, let's assume in a hawk-dove game that the larger bird always wins a fight. Our intuition is that we should then play hawk when confronting a smaller bird and dove when faced with a larger one. This is a sensible strategy: flee from larger birds and fight with smaller ones. By contrast, a paradoxical strategy is to fight with larger birds and flee from smaller ones. It sounds strange, but if all members of a population adhered to the paradoxical strategy of flying away when the opposing bird is smaller, then a sensible bird could not invade a population of paradoxical birds.

To prove this, consider what would happen if a sensible bird of average size entered a population of ten paradoxical birds. The sensible bird would flee from encounters with half of the paradoxical birds (those that are larger). The sensible bird would fight with the other half of the paradoxical birds (those that are smaller), and both parties would incur injuries. Hence, the injury rate for the sensible bird would be one out of two confrontations with a paradoxical bird. Among the ten paradoxical birds, half would suffer harm from an encounter with the sensible bird. Assuming a ratio of ten to one paradoxical to sensible birds, the injury rate of the average paradoxical bird would be one in twenty encounters, or half of one out of every ten encounters with a sensible bird. The sensible bird's significantly higher incidence of injury would impair its ability to procreate, and it would soon die out within the population of paradoxical birds.

Some spiders exhibit paradoxical behavior.[23] If driven out of their nest by a predator, certain species of spiders will seek refuge by invading the nest of a nearby spider. Rather than fight, the spider whose nest has been invaded will immediately vacate their home and move to the nest of another spider. As one spider displaces another, an entire community of spiders, within moments, will have shifted to new abodes. Because the invading spider always plays hawk and the defending spider always responds with dove, no spider is ever harmed by another spider.

Fortunately, spiders seem to be quite happy, unlike most humans, with time-shares, and at least one spider, the last to relocate, must like living outdoors without a nest over its head.

Computer Programs Are Easily Identified

The iterated game of the prisoner's dilemma played in Axelrod's tournament assumed the programs played each other for extended periods of time, over hundreds of rounds. The programs "knew" whether the opponent cooperated or defected in the last round. This sometimes occurs in the biological world.

Vampire bats remember which of their fellow bats have shared blood with them in the past. To sustain themselves, vampire bats fly around at night to feed on the blood of various animals. On many evenings, a bat will be unable to find nourishment and will return starving. However, when a bat extracts blood from an animal, it builds a surplus of blood within its gut that can be shared with others. This sharing of blood by regurgitation from the fortunate to the less fortunate vampire bats within a cave is common. However, vampire bats taken from a distant cave and mixed with another community will not feed other bats within their new home.[24]

But in many cases, organisms confront each other only once. You cannot play TFT if there are no subsequent encounters. Moreover, in nature it may be difficult to readily identify an opponent. Just like in a one-round game of the prisoner's dilemma in which the optimal strategy is to defect, the ESS in a series of random one-off encounters in a hawk-dove game is to play hawk. This is particularly true between species, especially between a diner and those on the menu. In the example of lions and gazelles, the very nature of their relationship means there is no opportunity for either to play a TFT.

Overall, because of the confounding factors of sharing some of the same genes, asymmetrical payoffs, death as an outcome of a single encounter, and identification issues, JMS found that strict TFT behavior was not as widespread as he expected among living organisms. The behavior of insects, fish, and other animals often did not exhibit TFT. He realized that an ESS in the biological world followed more complex and nuanced rules than Axelrod's computer tournament.

Consequently, JMS concluded that TFT was frequently not the best strategy for many living organisms. In fact, he found more examples of defection than cooperation. When an ESS did emerge, it often deviated from the predictions of game theory, as modeled in Axelrod's tournament. Unable to find a uniform and widespread optimal strategy that was an ESS for many species in the insect, fish, or animal world, JMS turned his attention to another area within biology that had remained largely unexplained.

JMS sought to apply game theory and ESS to sex.

Sex: Hidden in Darkness

Merriam-Webster's dictionary defines sex as "either of the two major forms of individuals that occur in many species and that are distinguished respectively as female or male especially on the basis of their reproductive organs and structures."[25]

But reproductive organs and structures are not a determinant of sex. Frogs, sharks, and spiders have no penises.[26] Plants have varying kinds of flowers, fruits, and seeds.[27] In the animal kingdom, males and females can be distinguished by only one consistent physical difference: the sex cells of females are larger than those of males.[28] Additionally, female sex cells are almost always less numerous, as there is a trade-off between producing a larger size versus a larger number of sex cells, given limited caloric resources.[29]

Consider *Homo sapiens*. Female sex cells (eggs) are more than ten thousand times larger than male sex cells (sperms).[30] A healthy human male produces more than five hundred million sperm cells per day; the average human female releases about four hundred mature eggs over her lifetime.[31] In this regard, humans are typical of the animal world, in which there is a significant difference in the size and number of female and male sex cells. But it is not readily apparent why millions of years of evolution would have yielded such extreme divergences between the size and number of sex cells in females and males.

The substantial difference in the number of sex cells produced by males and females suggests that relatively few males would be required for a species to grow in numbers. Yet most multicellular creatures are known to have a ratio of males to females of approximately one to one.[32] Communities of mostly females would seem to be superior, at least in evolutionary terms. Assuming one child per female per generation, a population with a ten to one ratio of females to males could produce ten children per generation compared with just five in a community evenly split between males and females. More than a few males would seem to be an evolutionary waste of space.

It is also not clear why evolution overwhelmingly favored sexual reproduction at all. JMS wrote that sexual reproduction had a "two-fold disadvantage" over asexual reproduction.[33] As an example of the first disadvantage, JMS compared a population that procreated asexually (all self-fertilizing females) with one split evenly between males and females.[34] Assuming the same number of children per mother, the all-mother group will have twice as many babies. And beyond one generation, the disadvantage of sexual reproduction would grow exponentially because of compounding.

A second disadvantage according to JMS is that sexual reproduction requires effort and entails risks. Much time is spent evaluating, persuading, and then breeding with another creature—an expenditure of scarce resources that could be better employed searching for food or escaping predators. In some species, the competition for mates among males can lead to injury or even death. The sex act can also transmit diseases. The above could be avoided with asexual reproduction. Therefore, it would seem evolution should have gotten rid of males and replaced them with self-fertilizing females a long time ago.

Yet most animals and plants reproduce sexually.[35] Among vertebrates, less than 1 percent depend on asexual reproduction.[36]

Even Charles Darwin found the widespread prevalence of sex perplexing: "We do not even in the least know the final cause of sexuality; why new beings should be produced by the union of two sexual elements. The whole subject is as yet hidden in darkness."[37]

Since Darwin, biologists and others have struggled to explain why the process of natural selection has yielded vast differences in the size and number of female and male sex cells, an equal number of males and females in most multicellular organisms, and the widespread use of sexual reproduction. JMS, in his landmark book *The Evolution of Sex*, tackled these questions head-on. What he discovered was that game theory and ESS can explain a great deal about sex.

The Sexual Trade-Off: Size versus Number

The difference in the size and number of male and female sex cells is the result of an ESS in most species between these two types of cells.

When the first multicellular organisms began replicating, each type of sex cell would have been produced in roughly comparable quantities and would have been approximately the same size, as the genes for producing those sex cells were initially identical. However, over time, mutations eventually led to small differences between sex cells. Some sex cells were smaller and thus could be produced in greater numbers; others were larger but more limited in quantity.

Once these divergences appeared, an average-sized sex cell was at an evolutionary disadvantage. The smaller sex cells stood a greater chance of penetrating other sex cells, as they were more numerous. The larger sex cells had higher odds of surviving, since they contained more energy for nourishment to sustain themselves. Over time, average-sized sex cells lost the evolutionary struggle against smaller, more numerous sex cells and larger, more long-lived sex cells.

As average-sized sex cells died out, two distinct lines of genes developed: one for smaller sex cells and the other for larger ones. Over millions of generations, these two distinct sets of genes for sex cells steadily diverged. Smaller sex cells (sperms) became ever smaller to exploit the advantage of greater numbers. Larger sex cells (eggs) evolved to become even larger to capitalize on the benefit of a higher survival rate. Eventually, sperms and eggs reached a stage where the benefit of greater size or greater number reversed. Sperms stopped shrinking when the advantages of greater numbers were more than offset by a shorter life; eggs ceased swelling once the advantages of larger size were outweighed by a smaller number of cells. At this point, an ESS was established, and the size and number of male and female sex cells stopped fluctuating.

The optimal size and number of male and female sex cells differ for each species and can be disturbed by environmental factors that tip the trade-off between more cells versus longer life in one direction or the other. Nevertheless, in most species an ESS between sex cells was established: no mutant strategy, such as the introduction of an average-sized sex cell, could invade a population of existing sperms and eggs. A cell between the ESS size of a sperm and egg for a given species was either not numerous enough or not sufficiently long-lived to spread throughout a population.

The ESS of sex was launched by tiny, almost indiscernible mutations in the first sex cells. Just a slight difference in size and number of the first sex cells billions of years ago has yielded in most species two sexes: male and female.

Sexual Reproduction: Alice and Red Queens

Sexual reproduction also has an advantage over asexual reproduction in that it yields fewer harmful and more beneficial mutations.

Sexual reproduction reduces the number of harmful mutations by limiting inbreeding. If both sets of genes are from the same self-fertilizing mother, then there is a greater risk that life-threatening mutations could arise. Sexual reproduction also increases the number of beneficial mutations, as offspring inherit two different sets of genes. One analogy is a lottery in which you can either buy one hundred tickets with the same number or fifty tickets with numbers that differ. If you know the winning number, then the former strategy is better. If the winning number is uncertain, then the chances of winning improve with the latter strategy even though you have only half as many tickets.

Asexual reproduction is like buying one hundred tickets with the same number: if the future environment is known, then place all your money and all your genes on one outcome. Sexual reproduction is the equivalent of purchasing fifty tickets with different numbers: if the future environment is uncertain, then it is better to diversify your bets, even though only half of your genes will be carried into the next generation.[38] Given a constantly changing world, including food sources and predators, it is better to spread your genetic bets.

Sexual reproduction also enables the beneficial mutations of two individuals to be shared with their descendants. If person A and person B each have a distinct and separate gene for a physical characteristic that is advantageous for reproduction, then cross-breeding allows the children of A and B to inherit both traits. By contrast, asexual reproduction limits the spread of beneficial mutations. If A and B breed asexually, then the best each can do is to pass on their own unique advantageous genes to their respective offspring.

The ability to adapt to a changing environment and share beneficial mutations has been crucial to the survival of many animals, including *Homo sapiens*. This ability is particularly important to a host organism that must fight off parasites with a higher mutation rate. In a world filled with hostile organisms, such as those that cause diseases, the higher rate of mutation that arises from genetic diversity can be the difference between life and death.

Diseases attack by either invading healthy cells to eat them (bacteria) or hijacking healthy cell replication to make more diseased cells (viruses). To accomplish either one of the above, diseased cells must break through outer cell membranes to gain access to healthy cells. These outer cell membranes can be thought of as the equivalent of secure doors through which diseases attempt to enter.[39] Because diseased cells are constantly inventing new keys, healthy cells continually change the locks. The faster the rate of evolution of diseased cells, the greater the chance of opening an outer membrane door of a healthy cell. Diseased cells can replicate in minutes; a new generation of humans takes many years. Compared with asexual reproduction, sexual reproduction yields more genetic diversity, which helps offset the inability of most animals to evolve at a faster rate than diseased cells. Sexual reproduction is a quicker way to change the locks.

This has been proven empirically: asexual species, mainly microscopic organisms and insects, evolve rapidly and are largely disease free.[40] By contrast, animals that evolve at a much slower rate, such as *Homo sapiens*, frequently succumb to illness before dying of old age. Sexual reproduction is a way to partially compensate for the faster rate at which diseases evolve compared with their animal hosts.

The idea that sex provides a means for organisms to readily adapt to a changing, hostile environment has been called the Red Queen hypothesis. In Lewis Carroll's *Through the Looking-Glass*, Alice encounters a chess game in which one of the animated pieces, a Red Queen, takes the young girl on a chase that leads them nowhere. The Red Queen explains to Alice: "Now, here, you see, it takes all the running you can do, to keep in the same place. If you want to get somewhere else, you must run at least twice as fast as that."[41] A species such as *Homo sapiens* must constantly evolve just to stay alive, given a changing physical environment and competing hostile organisms. In the analogy of Alice and the Red Queen, human hosts have to reproduce with twice as much genetic diversity just to keep up with more rapidly replicating parasites.

The Battle of the Sexes[42]

The advantages of sexual reproduction come at a cost: the interests of males and females are not aligned. The basic conflict between males and females is over who is left "holding the baby." Mothers and fathers have an incentive to ensure offspring reach reproductive age and pass on their respective genes. However, after the child is born, the mother or father has the option to defect by deserting the baby to go off and mate with another.

The parent that deserts first will force the parent left behind into a cruel choice: abandon the baby, increasing the odds it will die, or care for the child until it reaches reproductive age. In most cases, the parent left holding the baby is better off investing their time and effort in the existing child rather than deserting the newborn; otherwise they would have to find another mate and start the reproductive process all over again. Meanwhile, the deserting parent can immediately devote all their energies into procreating again. As a result, the parent who deserts first will have more offspring, and the genes for deserting first will rapidly spread throughout a population.

But it is not quite that simple. The sex that emerges victorious in this battle of the sexes varies by species and is partly determined by how babies are made.

Internal and External Fertilization: Mommy versus Daddy Care

Maternal care is common in species that procreate through internal fertilization.[43] This method of reproduction is most typical of land-dwelling animals, as the fertilized egg of a land-dwelling animal must be bathed in the internal fluids of the mother to survive. In these cases, the male has the option to desert first, after copulation; the female must then decide to either desert the baby or care for the newborn.

On the other hand, paternal care is common among fish, who reproduce through external fertilization. A female spews her eggs into the water, and the male can then choose whether to fertilize the eggs. Unlike mammals, the sex cells of many female fish are viable in water and outside the body of the mother. But fish sperms are lighter and at greater risk of being swept away once released. By contrast, fish eggs are heavier and more likely to remain together in the water as a clutch.

If the male releases sperm first, then he risks having his sperms drift away before the female spews her eggs. Therefore, the female can spawn first, knowing the male will wait for her to do so to make sure that his sperms will not drift away before penetrating her eggs. The female can spawn and then immediately swim away, leaving the male holding the baby. Hence, the battle of the sexes between male and female fish over who deserts first favors the female because of the timing of the release of sperms and eggs and external gestation.[44] As a result, of the estimated 30 percent of fish species that provide parental care, 78 percent of the time this care is by one parent, usually the male.[45]

In terms of parental care, the ESS that has evolved between males and females on land and in water differs significantly. In land-dwelling mammals, females almost always provide the care alone or in groups (humans are a rare exception).[46] Many species of fish who procreate through external fertilization practice paternal care.[47] In addition, the few species of fish that have transitioned between internal and external fertilization have demonstrated a consistent pattern: a move from external to internal fertilization typically results in a switch from paternal to maternal care.[48] Conversely, a change from internal to external fertilization usually causes a shift from maternal to paternal care.[49]

Mother's Baby, Father's Maybe

Another factor in the battle of the sexes is the issue of paternity. Females have a strong motivation to care for and to defend their offspring: every mother knows her baby carries half her genes. However, in the case of internal fertilization, the male has less certainty about the genetics of his family, as he does not know with certainty where the female has been spending her time away. On the other hand, in the instance of external fertilization, males have greater certainty of paternity, as they release sperms over unfertilized eggs. This is another reason that paternal care is frequently practiced in water but rarely on land.[50]

Pregnancy: The Great Contraceptive

In the battle of the sexes, the females of some species have a significant disadvantage: long gestation periods. This is particularly true among mammals. For example, female elephants are pregnant for twenty-two months and able to produce offspring only about once every four years.[51] During these gestation periods, male elephants can continue to mate. In addition, in many species, lactation prevents conception.

Pregnancy and nourishment of newborns prevents many females from reproducing for extended periods. Males have no such constraints.

Males Compete Rather Than Care

The ability to leave and procreate with other females means that males whose genes favor desertion will have more offspring. Males often do not provide parental care in species with internal fertilization and long gestation periods. Therefore, natural selection in land animals often favors males that spend more time competing for females and less time on parenting.[52] In 90 percent of mammals, females provide all or most of the parental care.[53]

The evolutionary advantage also goes to males who develop the physical characteristics that allow them to gain access to females, beating out males who develop features for tending to offspring. While mothers often have specific glands for nourishment (breasts), fathers generally exhibit physical characteristics for competition (greater size). This was particularly true in the first several million years of the existence of our species. It is estimated that males of the hominid species that led to *Homo sapiens* were on average 50 percent heavier than females.[54]

In addition, natural selection will most often favor males whose genes produce behaviors more suitable for competition with other males than for providing paternal care. This may explain why males on average are more aggressive. In one survey, men were the perpetrators of 86 percent of all violent crime in the United States.[55]

Natural selection will similarly encourage a greater degree of indiscriminate sexuality in males compared with females. In a study at Florida State University, attractive undergraduate female student volunteers approached students of the opposite sex who were walking alone and said, "Hi, I've noticed you around town lately, and I find you very attractive. Would you go to bed with me tonight?"[56] About 75 percent of the young men said yes. When the roles were reversed, not one of the young female undergraduates accepted an offer from an attractive male.[57] Males in the United States spend more money each year at strip clubs than on tickets to Broadway, off-Broadway, regional theater, the opera, ballet, jazz, and classical music performances combined.[58]

The philosopher Jerry Seinfeld has said:

> *The basic conflict between men and women, sexually, is that men are firemen. To men, sex is an emergency, and no matter what we're doing we can be ready in two minutes. Women, on the other*

hand, are like fire. They're very exciting, but condi-
tions have to be exactly right for it to occur.[59]

Terrible Fathers but Good Donors

Since paternal care is so unreliable, female land-based animals attempt to make the best of a bad situation by picking fathers with good genes. While males may not be very useful in terms of the care and feeding of the brood, at least they can contribute physical traits that aid in the survival of their offspring. Therefore, land-based mothers are often choosy about their mates, selecting those with physical signs of good survival genes.

An example of this is peahens.

Peahens are attracted to peacocks with a larger train and a greater number of eyespots. But a heavier and more brightly colored tail poses a greater risk of predation, reducing the survival rates for a peacock. Darwin himself was so troubled by this glaring exception to his theory of evolution that he wrote in April 1860 that the sight of a peacock tail "makes me sick!"[60]

Darwin attempted to explain the peacock's tail as a matter of aesthetics:

> *A girl sees a handsome man and without observ-*
> *ing whether his nose or his whiskers are a tenth of*
> *an inch longer or shorter than in some other man,*
> *admires his appearance and says she will marry*
> *him. So, I suppose with the peahen; and the tail has*
> *been increased in length merely by on the whole*
> *presenting a more gorgeous appearance.*[61]

Later in life, Darwin would suggest a more convincing argument that showed how his thinking had evolved:

> *I feel very doubtful about the share males and females play in sexual selection; I suspect that the male will pair with any female, and that females select the most victorious or most beautiful cock, or him with beauty and courage combined.*[62]

The idea of a "most victorious" peacock indicates Darwin realized that a larger and brighter tail was a handicap that only the strongest and fittest male could overcome. An analogy is to a runner who is able to win the race despite carrying a backpack of rocks. A larger and brighter tail is a sign that a peacock's genes are superior, given that he has not been eaten by a predator despite the obvious handicap.

However, a larger and brighter tail hinders the defense of peachicks. The large and colorful tail means that a peacock cannot move quickly, and he attracts the attention of predators—both of which endanger newly hatched birds. (This is why a peahen's tail is smaller and largely colorless.) For a peacock, signaling the possession of superior genes and thereby gaining access to the limited supply of peahen eggs is more important than protecting peachicks.

Once begun, the cycle of generations of peahens favoring the most handicapped peacocks could not be stopped. Within a given population, it is estimated that 5 percent of peacocks typically constitute the majority of mates of peahens.[63] Thus, only a small fraction of males—those with the greatest handicaps, such as large and brightly colored tails—were selected to be fathers by peahens. This leads to larger and brighter peacock tails with each successive generation.

Compounding this effect is evidence in many species of what biologists call "linkage disequilibrium."[64] In the case of peacocks, this is another way of saying that genes for long tails and genes for preferring males with long tails are tied together. The idea is that if I am a peacock with a long tail, that is because my mother picked a father with a long tail, which demonstrates that my mother had genes with a preference for peacocks with long tails. Consequently, genes in peacocks for long tails and genes in peahens for preferring peacocks with long tails become linked together over subsequent generations, carried forward within the bodies of both males and females. For peahens, genes for long tails are expressed through a behavioral tendency to choose peacocks with long tails as mates. This preference is then passed on to future generations of daughters.

Harems: Good for Alpha Males but Not the Kids

The lack of peacock involvement with the peachicks is not much different from that of other land-based males. However, land-based females have developed strategies to encourage, as best they can, males to care for their offspring. This is particularly critical in the animal world, in which a few males tend to dominate other members of the group.

A survey of thirteen primate species concluded that the alpha male of the group sired on average two out of three of all offspring in the group.[65] One study estimated that among *Homo sapiens* in prehistoric times about 80 percent of women were mothers but only 40 percent of men were able to become fathers.[66] This results in a different kind of ESS: only the fittest and most forceful males are able to procreate.

To illustrate the effect of an alpha male on childcare, consider the example of a group of ten males and ten females in which the alpha male sires all the offspring. To the extent he expends any effort at all, the alpha male will spread his paternal care across his offspring from the ten mothers. Nine of ten males have no reason to devote any time or effort on parental care since none of the children are theirs.

Of course, each of the ten mothers will devote all their energies to their own children. By contrast, in a monogamous community, all ten males will devote time and effort to the care of their own children. Hence, the net effect of the presence of an alpha male will be less time and effort spent by males on childcare. Nevertheless, from the perspective of the alpha male, the optimal ESS is one in which he alone sires offspring. From the viewpoint of the females, the optimal ESS is one of strict monogamy to incentivize each male to devote 100 percent of his time to the care of his children.

Despite this basic conflict between alpha males and females, there are reasons for the two genders to cooperate and declare periodic cease-fires in the battle of the sexes. The most important one relates to the advantages of a division of labor when parenting.

Two-Parent Households Are Better

In many species, especially in the animal kingdom, survival rates are largely a function of parental care.

The expenditure of time and effort to ensure progeny reach reproductive age can be broken down into two broad categories: nourishment and defense.[67] Given these two separate and distinct functions, there are advantages to specialization between parents: one can feed the kids while the other is fighting off predators. In addition, the physical characteristics best suited for care and defense differ. Thus, those who have two parents are more likely to survive. One study of a modern hunter-gatherer community in Paraguay found that the mortality of children more than doubled when a father was not present.[68]

Male-dominated polygamy is best for the dominant male but not for the group on average: the ten females each receive only one-tenth of the paternal care of the dominant male, and the other nine males, who are childless, spend no time or effort on the offspring of the dominant male. By contrast, under monogamy, the ten females would each receive the full-time parental care of a male, and the other nine males get to be fathers.

As you have probably already guessed, the strategies of caring and deserting have parallels to the prisoner's dilemma. Caring is the equivalent of cooperating on parental care; deserting is the same as defecting by not cooperating after the child is born. While deserting is in the best interests of the alpha male, the group as a whole is worse off, as the overall level of childcare declines.

Ducks, Sticklebacks, Fruit Flies, and Gibbons

JMS recognized the parallels between the battle of the sexes and the prisoner's dilemma. In *The Evolution of Sex*, he cast the conflict between males and females into terms of "guard" or "desert." JMS labeled four possible ESSs with animal names, each signifying a type of parental care: Duck (male deserts, female guards), Stickleback (male guards, female deserts), Fruit Fly (both desert), and Gibbon (both guard).[69] JMS noted that Duck has been by far the dominant ESS among mammals, with few exceptions. Given internal fertilization and extended gestation periods, it is not surprising that males would desert. A better question is why Gibbon as a strategy has survived as an ESS in any mammal species.

Numerous theories have been put forward, but none have proven conclusive. One theory is that mammal species have a high rate of infanticide, and therefore both parents are required to guard the children. A research study concluded that among 260 species of mammals, 119 regularly practiced infanticide.[70] However, the same study noted that species such as lions and baboons, which use a Duck strategy, have higher rates of infanticide than humans, who employ Gibbon.[71]

Another theory is that over the course of evolutionary history some mammals, such as humans, were widely dispersed. Without ready access to new females, there was an incentive for a male to stay with a female, as investing in the survival of his existing offspring was more productive than searching for new females in distant lands to impregnate. A Gibbon strategy could simply be the result of a lack of available females.

An example of this can be found in the American West when it was first settled. In 1859, it was estimated that there was one woman for every two hundred men in the territory west of the Missouri River.[72] Surveys indicate that marriages in the American West at that time were more likely to be "egalitarian power relationships."[73] The western states enfranchised women long before women in the eastern states got the right to vote, demonstrating that frontier women had more political and social clout than their city counterparts.[74] Not surprisingly, women can demand more when there is a surplus of men. Those demands include parental care and fidelity.

But the skewed sex ratio of the American West in the nineteenth century is a product of a particular time and place in history. We do not actually know whether there were similar disparities due to environmental conditions in our distant past. A comprehensive study of thousands of multicellular organisms demonstrated that biparental care throughout evolutionary history has lasted only for short periods of time.[75] This study confirmed the basic theory behind the conflict between males and females: each has an incentive to desert first. The study concluded:

> *Once evolved, biparental care shows high rates of transition back towards male only or female only care, indicating that it is an evolutionary unstable condition . . . due to the different costs of care between the sexes and selection for desertion. Our results strongly indicate that biparental care, in whatever form it arises, is an evolutionary unstable condition that is quickly lost.*[76]

Humans are clearly an exception to the above—today, we are predominately a monogamous species, and despite the evolutionary forces pushing a Duck strategy, most humans practice Gibbon. That makes humans one of the few exceptions to the rule among species that procreate through internal fertilization and undergo extended gestation periods.

Monogamy and the Invasive Strategy of Polygamy

It is unknown whether humans have been largely monogamous or polygamous throughout our time on Earth. Humans split off from an ancient ancestor shared with today's chimpanzees about seven million years ago. If human evolution was compressed into a single calendar year, we lived in small hunter-gatherer communities until 9:00 a.m. on December 31. These hunter-gatherer communities typically comprised about forty to one hundred men, women, and children.[77] Hunter-gatherers roamed most of the continents of the world, foraging for plants, fruits, and nuts and hunting wild animals. Contact between geographically dispersed small bands of hunter-gatherers was limited. Until the Agricultural Revolution, which began in the Middle East around twelve thousand years ago, most humans, most of the time, were born, mated, and died within the same small group of individuals, all known to each other.

Individuals within small hunter-gatherer communities could practice either monogamy or polygamy. These two strategies have parallels with the prisoner's dilemma.

In a monogamous tribe, males are certain of paternity, do not need to compete for females once they find a mate, and should care for their offspring. Males would have an additional incentive to provide childcare because they cannot pursue additional mates among a population of monogamous females. By contrast, in a polygamous community, males will question paternity and must compete for reproductive resources, so time is better spent on trying to copulate with females rather than looking after the needs of the newborn.

Therefore, a monogamous community will devote the most time and effort to childcare, as males do not waste energy competing with each other for females and instead focus their attention on parenting. This is the equivalent in the prisoner's dilemma to mutual cooperation. By contrast, in a polygamous community with dominant alpha males, most males will have no incentive to invest in parental care, and females will receive only a portion of their mate's attention. This is comparable to mutual defection in the prisoner's dilemma.

But monogamy is a strategy that is subject to being invaded by polygamy. Suppose that several females and males, unbeknownst to their fellow community members, switch to polygamy. Some unsuspecting males will devote all their energies to care of the children of other men. Meanwhile, the polygamous males will spend their time trying to mate with polygamous females, with the result that the males will have more children, and genes for polygamy will spread throughout the population. Thus, it seems that polygamy would be the only ESS.

However, this outcome directly contradicts the modern history of human sexual relations. Monogamy and biparental care have been, by far, the most common type of sexual relationships practiced by humans, at least during recorded history.

But human behavior, including sexual relations between males and females, is not determined solely by the urge to procreate and evolutionary pressures. Our large, complex brains mediate many basic animal instincts and regularly interfere with the forces of natural selection. If genes ran our lives, then it would be hard to explain the invention and widespread use of birth control.

Even JMS admitted that concerning the sexual activities of humans, "these models [are] insubstantial and unsatisfactory. But they are the best we have."[78]

The Future of Sex

I believe monogamy and biparental care will continue to be the norm for *Homo sapiens* for the foreseeable future. But conditions on the ground in the battle of the sexes are rapidly changing.

First, human males today can find new mates without undertaking treacherous journeys to the next valley, which may be populated with more hungry saber-toothed tigers than unaccompanied, fertile human females. The availability of mates and the ability to cheat without detection are significantly greater now than at any time before in our evolutionary history.

Second, parental care no longer strongly correlates with survival rates. In the past, care by at least one parent was necessary for a child to live long enough to reproduce. Today, abandoned children in most nations are raised by state or private institutions.

Third, contraceptives allow males and females much greater choice in reproduction. For seven million years, sex consistently yielded progeny. Today, children are optional.

Fourth, a mom and a dad increasingly are also becoming optional. Same-sex marriages are not uncommon and, with the help of modern science, can produce biological offspring.

One can peer out over the horizon into the future and imagine a different outcome in the battle of the sexes. The new conditions on the ground are unlike any under which males and females have competed in the past. Therefore, we should not expect the same result.

In my view, the battle of the sexes over who deserts first will be less fiercely fought in the future. A child who is supported by one or both parents may have greater benefits, such as a better education or improved social status. But in terms of passing on genes through offspring to subsequent generations, parental care has become less important. Women have more control over their bodies. Mates are easier to find. Opposite-sex parents are not the only pairings.

Because of this combination of factors, females may have less interest in monogamy in the years ahead. Many males never did.

Conclusions

The battle of the sexes continues to be waged throughout the biological world. As we have seen, there are no simple answers to the mysteries of reproduction. In many ways, we are fortunate to be one of the few species experiencing a truce in the battle of the sexes in which males and females largely cooperate to raise our young. We have established an ESS based on monogamy and biparental care that is the norm across much of the planet. Most *Homo sapiens* men and women have decided to cooperate. At least for now.

The battle of the sexes is an example of a prisoner's dilemma of who deserts first played out across millions of years between billions of couples. But the most famous example of the prisoner's dilemma, known as mutual assured destruction, or MAD for short, is less than eight decades old.

Without question, MAD is the most consequential game of prisoner's dilemma that has ever been played. Since 1945, we have hoped that the two main players in this game will continue to act rationally. But the man most commonly associated with the proposition that a nuclear war is winnable was not so sure.

In fact, he thought MAD was insane.

CHAPTER 5

Mutual Assured Destruction: Suicide for Peace

Herman Kahn: Intellect, Enthusiasm, and LSD

Herman Kahn (1922–1983) was a military strategist and futurist who founded the Hudson Institute, a policy research organization.[1] He was best known for his writings on nuclear war and served as a source of inspiration for the character of Dr. Strangelove in the movie of the same name.

Kahn was born in New Jersey, the middle son of poor immigrants, and his parents divorced when he was ten. His mother moved the children to Los Angeles, where the family lived on public assistance and Kahn worked odd jobs from a young age. He enrolled at the University of Southern California and then transferred to the University of California, Los Angeles (UCLA) as a physics major. During World War II, he was drafted into the Army Reserve Corps. As part of the induction process, Kahn was required to take the Army General Classification Test, a measure of IQ. The sergeant proctoring the exam warned the inductees not to worry about answering all the questions on the forty-five-minute exam because "no one has ever finished."[2] Kahn completed the exam in twenty minutes and received the highest score ever recorded on the test up to that time.[3]

Kahn was sent to Texas for basic training and afterward was offered jobs at Los Alamos working on the Manhattan Project and in the Signal Corps overseas. However, the offer at Los Alamos came with no job description, because of security restrictions, and so Kahn turned it down. He was then posted to Burma (now Myanmar), where he operated the signals line between China and Rangoon (now known as Yangon). In 1946, after demobilization, Kahn reenrolled at UCLA and completed his bachelor of science degree. Kahn's math professor said he was his brightest student in twenty-five years. In 1947, Kahn earned a master's in physics from the California Institute of Technology and after graduation took a job at RAND Corporation. The RAND division head who hired him said, "This guy is a genius or crazy. We'll see."[4]

Kahn worked at the military think tank until 1961. His first project at RAND was to design a nuclear-powered airplane. While he was unsuccessful (the idea was totally impractical), the project brought his talents to the attention of others at RAND, and he was transferred to the hydrogen bomb project, where he worked with Edward Teller. Although his activities on the hydrogen bomb project remain classified, it has been reported that Kahn contributed to the design of one of the earliest thermonuclear weapons.[5]

While at RAND, Kahn befriended the economist Andrew Marshall, and soon the two were collaborating. In 1952, Kahn coauthored with Marshall the first systems analysis of bombing raids against the Soviet Union. Kahn was hooked. The next two decades of his life would be spent thinking about warfare, and he left physics behind.

Kahn was popular with the Air Force officers who traveled to RAND's Santa Monica headquarters to attend briefings on military strategy. Unlike other RAND researchers, he did not read from a text or refer to notes. He had a near photographic memory and prepared lectures in his head. His seminars were frequently two six-hour talks given without interruption, split over two successive days. He spoke rapidly, pacing back and forth, hands in the air, gesturing toward one of the hundreds of charts and graphs flashing rapidly across screens at the front of the room. And he enlivened his lectures with stories and sarcastic humor.

Kahn once told an audience of military officers: "We take God's view. The President's view. Big. Aerial. Global. Galactic. Ethereal. Spatial. Megalomania is the standard occupational hazard."[6] He did not fear challenging military commanders who disagreed with him. In one heated exchange, Kahn said, "Colonel, how many thermonuclear wars have you fought? Our research shows that you need to fight a dozen or so to begin to get the feel for it."[7] Kahn was also a fierce and confident debater. He had a favorite saying after listening to an opposing point of view: "I can make your argument better than you can, and then I can show you why it's wrong."[8]

Much to the dismay of the military, Kahn was known to enjoy the company of a wide range of people. He was fascinated by the counterculture of the 1960s and dropped acid with Abbie Hoffman. As Kahn told a reporter, "I like hippies. I've been to Esalen. I've had LSD a couple of times. In some ways I'd like to join them."[9] He also spent days talking with various peace activists, including those on the Committee for Non-Violent Action, the National Committee for a Sane Nuclear Policy, and other well-known anti-war groups. He pursued meetings with religiously oriented pacifists such as the Quakers. He appeared at a peace rally with beat poet Allen Ginsberg. The US government actually revoked Kahn's security clearance for two years because of these contacts.

In 1961, Kahn moved to New York and founded the Hudson Institute, what he called a "high-class RAND." Kahn would remain its chair and director of research until his death.[10] Under his leadership, the Hudson Institute grew into an international think tank with offices across the globe.

From 1966 to 1968, Kahn was heavily involved in the Vietnam War as an advisor to the US Department of Defense. He coined the phrase "Vietnamization," which he said is "a better word than de-Americanization which has the connotation of running away."[11] He thought the Vietnam War was not cost-effective, "sending a $5 million aircraft with $5,000 bombs to maybe hit a $1,000 truck."[12] He believed the US policy throughout the Vietnam War of selective bombing of North Vietnamese targets was pointless—either drop enough munitions to force an immediate surrender or do not fight at all. Even then, he was skeptical about the prospects for victory, noting that

> more than half the average everyday Vietnamese peasants, I guess, are VC or VC sympathizers. . . . The average North Vietnamese soldier has less than a year to live. They sing a song, "Born in the North, Die in the South." . . . The people are willing. They can send down 50,000 soldiers every year for the rest of history.[13]

During the 1970s, Kahn expanded his work at the Hudson Institute to include forecasting global trends. He got some things wrong (the rapid colonization of space) but more things right (the rise of the Japanese and Korean economies, the development of high-strength and light structural materials, and new sources of power for electricity and automobiles). Kahn weighed more than three hundred pounds for most of his adult life, refused to exercise or diet, and died of a stroke at sixty-one. It was appropriate that in his last few days he was working on a presentation to be delivered at the Pentagon on nuclear warfare.

Upon hearing the news of Kahn's death, then-president Ronald Reagan said about the man who had given briefings on nuclear security to every commander in chief since Truman:

> [He] brought the lessons of science, history, and humanity to the study of the future and remained confident of mankind's potential for good. All who value independent thinking will mourn the loss of a man whose intellect and enthusiasm embraced so much.[14]

On Thermonuclear War

Kahn first became famous for his 1960 book, *On Thermonuclear War*.[15] Because of the success of the book, he was featured on various magazine covers and appeared on numerous television shows. The book even acquired its own acronym in popular culture: *OTW*. Kahn attracted the attention of director Stanley Kubrick, who subsequently made the popular 1964 film *Dr. Strangelove*. The film was inspired partly by Kahn's book and included a doomsday machine—a concept from the book—designed by the "BLAND Corporation."[16]

OTW was based on a little-noticed RAND paper that Kahn wrote in 1960, "The Nature and Feasibility of War and Deterrence."[17] In this paper, Kahn concluded that the US government's stated strategy concerning the use of nuclear weapons was fundamentally misguided and downright dangerous. This strategy, detailed in the US military's Single Integrated Operational Plan (SIOP), had only one response to any attack on the United States or its allies: a full-scale nuclear war.[18] For example, in response to a conventional attack on a North Atlantic Treaty Organization (NATO) ally, the 1962 SIOP specified that the United States launch 1,459 nuclear missiles at 654 military and civilian targets in the Soviet Union, Eastern Europe, and China. The range of targets went far beyond what was required for effective deterrence. The document detailing the SIOP ran to more than one million pages and included such "critical" targets as a single railroad bridge in Bulgaria.[19] The 1962 SIOP explicitly claimed not to target civilian populations but included hitting military installations within ten miles of the Kremlin with fifteen nuclear bombs, which would effectively kill most residents of Moscow.[20] In total, the 1962 SIOP, if implemented, would have resulted in the death of an estimated 285 million Russians and Chinese with hundreds of millions more deaths over time due to radioactive fallout.[21] As Kahn once told a group of Air Force generals, "Gentlemen, you don't have a war plan, you have a war-gasm."[22]

Rather than retaliate with a full-scale nuclear attack after the detonation of a single atomic bomb on US soil or an invasion by Soviet conventional forces of a European ally, Kahn believed the United States should adopt a Tit-for-Tat (TFT) strategy, escalating or deescalating our responses depending on the behavior of the Soviets. That included waging a conventional or limited nuclear war. In Kahn's view, the US military's SIOP guaranteed that any conflict between the two countries would escalate immediately to a full-scale nuclear war, foreclosing options for either country to back down. Kahn said that the United States had an inability to "think of nuclear war as an event. We think of it as the end of history."[23]

In *OTW*, Kahn wrote:

> *We must begin thinking of thermonuclear war as*
> *something which may be fought or deterred by*
> *an objective capability, rather than as a sort of*
> *nightmare which is banished by the possession*
> *in peacetime of a system that delivers bombs. . . .*
> *Our almost complete reliance on deterrence work-*
> *ing is probably an example of frivolity or wishful*
> *thinking.*[24]

Kahn's critics lashed out at him for proposing to fight a limited nuclear war with a TFT strategy. The review of *OTW* in the
March 1961 issue of *Scientific American* read, "This is a moral
tract on mass murder: How to plan it, how to commit it, how
to get away with it, how to justify it. . . . This evil and tenebrous
book is permeated with a bloodthirsty irrationality [and] . . .
obscene fantasies."[25] The *New Statesman* called it "pornography
for officers."[26]

At the time of *OTW*'s publication, the US policy of massive
retaliation with a full-scale nuclear strike contained in the SIOP
was known as "assured destruction." In 1962, an analyst working for Kahn at the Hudson Institute, Donald Brennan, coined
the term "mutual assured destruction" along with its acronym,
MAD. Brennan added the word mutual ironically to demonstrate
the absurdity of responding to any provocation with a full-scale
nuclear attack.[27]

Kahn and Brennan had similar views on MAD. Kahn wrote,
"The MAD policy fits its acronym: it is somewhat insane (and
immoral) to suggest that a nation should risk suicide in pursuit
of peace."[28]

A Crazy Strategy for an Insane World

MAD has been put forward as a classic prisoner's dilemma. All nations would prefer a world without nuclear weapons, which cost a lot and threaten to end life on Earth as we know it. However, a nation that lacks nuclear weapons is vulnerable, unless all other nuclear nations agree to disarm. So individual nations act in their own self-interest and acquire nuclear weapons even though collectively all nations are worse off.

But MAD is really two different games of the prisoner's dilemma played simultaneously.

The first game contained within MAD involves the stockpiling of nuclear weapons. In this game, nations can cooperate (agree to arms limitation treaties) or defect (build more bombs). This first game is played over decades with multiple opportunities to reward and punish moves by the other players. An arms race is more expensive for both sides, so the payoffs are measured in savings on military expenditures.

In this iterated game of the prisoner's dilemma, TFT is the optimal strategy. Defection on every move is possible but expensive and ultimately counterproductive, as the other side responds in kind and afterward neither side has an advantage, just a higher level of expenditures. Even with the benefit of a series of arms limitation agreements, the United States spent $5.5 trillion on nuclear weapons between 1940 and 1996.[29] The United States is expected to spend another $1.2 trillion over the next thirty years.[30] That money could rebuild a lot of schools, bridges, and airports.

For half a century, the United States and the Soviet Union/ Russian Federation played TFT strategies in this first game, starting with the Treaty on the Non-Proliferation of Nuclear Weapons (NPT) in 1968 and the Strategic Arms Limitation Talks (SALT I) in 1972. During the Cold War, nuclear arsenals totaled more than sixty thousand atomic bombs, almost entirely held by the

United States and the Soviet Union.[31] Today, there are an estimated 13,500 nuclear warheads globally, with the United States and Russia still leading the way with 5,550 and 6,375 nuclear weapons, respectively.[32] (The next largest nuclear power, China, possesses an estimated 320.[33]) The world today has nine nuclear powers—Russia, the United States, China, France, the United Kingdom, Pakistan, India, Israel, and North Korea. Three decades ago, this number was thirteen (South Africa, Ukraine, Kazakhstan, and Belarus no longer have atomic bombs). Somewhat paradoxically, the United States and Russia have actively discouraged other countries from acquiring nuclear weapons. The two opposing powers have worked together to limit the nuclear military might of their respective allies.

The second game contained within MAD concerns the use of nuclear weapons. In this game, cooperation by both players on the first and every subsequent move is the only strategy if nations are to survive a full-scale attack. There is no chance in this second game to play TFT: if a nation launches a full-scale first strike, MAD dictates that the defending nation immediately respond with a full-scale second strike. Mutual defection ends the game. Permanently. The fact that you are reading about nuclear war and the prisoner's dilemma is evidence that mutual cooperation has prevailed. (However, no one would be around after a full-scale global nuclear war to read about game theory, so this may just be a case of survivor bias. See my book *Fooled by the Winners* if you wish to travel down this epistemological rabbit hole.)

These two games of the prisoner's dilemma are similar in that in the end both are about the stockpiling and use of nuclear weapons. But the payoffs and optimal strategies (TFT and All Cooperate) for these interdependent games differ significantly. Hence the internal contradictions of MAD: leaders threaten each other with utter destruction while signing arms control agreements.

Strikes and Chickens

Kahn was the first to identify just how the dynamics of these two games of the MAD version of the prisoner's dilemma differed. As he often did, Kahn cast these two games in the form of memorable analogies.

Kahn said that the first game was comparable to the one played between labor and management. He wrote:

> *In a strike situation, labor and management threaten to inflict harm on each other, do so, and under pressure of the continuation of this harm, they seek agreement. It is usually assumed that events will not escalate to the limit (i.e., erupt): we do not expect workers to starve to death or businesses to go bankrupt.*[34]

A strike or management lockout is the equivalent of defection to punish the other side. In a strike, labor will forgo wages, and in a lockout, management will defer profits, even though both sides know eventually a settlement will be reached. A labor settlement is the same as cooperation. Both sides would be better off without a strike or a lockout, but each must be willing to incur losses occasionally to demonstrate bargaining resolve. Just as in an iterated game of the prisoner's dilemma, labor and management play TFT but typically lock in long cycles of cooperation, punctuated by occasional defections in the form of strikes and lockouts.

Similarly, in the first game of the nuclear prisoner's dilemma, nations expend funds on nuclear arsenals, incurring costs, as part of bargaining with other nations. Other nations respond in kind, but often there is a settlement, in the form of an arms treaty, before either country is bankrupted by military expenditures.

By contrast, the second game is quite different.

Kahn likened the second game to the one played by teenagers in 1950s movies—"chicken."[35] Kahn wrote:

> *Chicken is played by two drivers on a road with a white line down the middle. Both cars straddle the white line and drive toward each other at top speed. The first driver to lose his nerve and swerve into his own lane is "chicken"—an object of contempt and scorn—and he loses the game.*[36]

Kahn said that the best strategy in a game of chicken was for a driver to break off the steering wheel and hold it out the window in full view of the other driver, who then has only two choices: swerve or die. Kahn feared that the nuclear game of chicken could push either the United States or the Soviet Union into a preemptive strike—the equivalent of holding up the broken steering wheel for the other driver to see. Kahn worried that the "probability of war eventually occurring as a result of chicken being played once too often may be very high."[37]

Given the downside of playing chicken with thousands of nuclear devices, Kahn advocated in *OTW* that the United States adopt a TFT strategy in this second game of prisoner's dilemma. If the Soviets drop a nuclear bomb on Baltimore, then the United States should respond by destroying Novgorod and then wait to see what the Soviets do next.

But this was quite controversial. As discussed above, the US SIOP at the time Kahn wrote *OTW* called for a full-scale nuclear strike in response to any attack, conventional or nuclear, on the United States or its allies, regardless of magnitude. Kahn was proposing a fundamental shift in US nuclear strategy.

Further aggravating his critics, Kahn went on to detail a forty-four-step "escalation ladder" in his follow-up book to *OTW*, titled appropriately *On Escalation*, published in 1965.[38] The ladder begins with garden-variety political posturing (1. Ostensible Crisis), then moves through increasing levels of conflict (12. Large Conventional War), and eventually arrives at the complete annihilation of both countries (44. Spasm or Insensate War). Countries move up and down the ladder, playing TFT, seeking to lock in cooperation before multiple rounds of defection escalate to Step 44.

Kahn believed that TFT based on his escalation ladder offered the best chance for the United States (and the Soviet Union) to survive a nuclear war. He believed that a SIOP that limited the United States' options to a binary choice of no response or a full-scale attack was ill-considered and reckless.

To illustrate the flaws in the logic of MAD and US nuclear strategy, Kahn put forward the idea of a doomsday machine.

Doomsday Machine: Subject to Interpretation

Kahn wrote that MAD and US nuclear strategy depended on the absurd notion that "both of you believe that the other is willing to commit suicide . . . living out your lives happily and peacefully with only a slight twitch and regular fees to a psychoanalyst."[39]

The germ of the idea for a doomsday machine came from a science fiction novel, *Red Alert*, written by an ex–Royal Air Force officer. In the novel, the Soviets placed a couple dozen hydrogen bombs encased in cobalt that, upon detonation, would fatally poison all living creatures on Earth.

In 1959, Kahn coupled this idea with an automated computer system and labeled it a "Doomsday Machine."

> *Let us assume for 10 billion dollars one could build a device whose function is to destroy the world . . . connected to a computer, in turn connected to thousands of sensory devices. . . . The computer*

would be programmed so that if, say, five nuclear
bombs exploded over the United States, the device
would be triggered.[40]

Kahn also imagined that after the doomsday machine was completed, the United States would publish a "Soviet Criminal Code" to avoid misunderstandings. This code would list all the acts the Soviets were not allowed to commit. Kahn suggested that "the Soviets would be informed that if the computer detects them in any violation, it will blow away the world."[41] Kahn envisioned that in response the Soviets would build their own doomsday machine and publish a "United States Criminal Code," also in the interest of avoiding misunderstandings. Kahn concluded that a world with two doomsday machines and two criminal codes would not last long. He correctly pointed out that "the first time there is a difference in interpretation the world would be blown up."[42]

Kahn wrote about the idea of a doomsday machine to illustrate the absurdity of MAD. And then two decades later the Soviets built one.

Perimeter: A Very, Very Nice System

Perimeter is an automated nuclear weapon launch system used by the Russian Strategic Missile Forces.[43] After the United States installed Pershing II supersonic missiles in 1983 on German bases, the Soviets were concerned about whether their political and military leadership in Moscow could survive a first strike. In addition, the Chinese had deployed their first intercontinental ballistic missile (ICBM) near the Soviet border in 1981 and hinted at the possibility of launching a first strike against their neighbor. In response, the Soviets built Perimeter, which can trigger the launch of Russian ICBMs if the command-and-control structure of the Russian military is decapitated by a first strike. It is still functional today.

One of the principal designers of Perimeter, Valery Yarynich, a Soviet colonel, passed away in 2012. Before he died, he was asked in an interview why he participated in the construction of this doomsday machine. He replied: "The Perimeter system is very, very nice. We remove the unique responsibility from high politicians and the military. That is why we have the system."[44]

This was particularly important during times when Soviet leadership was incapacitated. In the year before his death in 1985, Soviet general secretary Konstantin Chernenko spent most of his time unable to walk, bedridden in a hospital, sometimes sedated.

But the Soviets did not publicly acknowledge that the Perimeter system existed until 2017, ten days after the confirmation of Donald Trump as president.[45] In an example of art anticipating life, the lead character in the 1964 movie *Dr. Strangelove* learns on the cusp of a US-Soviet nuclear war that the Soviet Union has built a doomsday device that will kill everyone on the planet in response to a first strike. Dr. Strangelove exclaims, "The whole point of a doomsday machine is lost if you keep it a secret! Why didn't you tell the world?" The Soviet ambassador shrugs his shoulders and says, "It was to be announced at the party congress on Monday."[46]

Other than Russia, no country has publicly acknowledged the existence of a doomsday machine. In stark contrast, the United States has opted for near-total transparency about our "dead hand" command-and-control systems.

From 1961 to 1990, twenty-four hours a day, seven days a week, the US Air Force flew in the skies over America at least one of a fleet of specially equipped planes capable of launching a nuclear attack. Known as Looking Glass, this backup system was designed to ensure that the United States could launch a counterattack. If the US ground command system is compromised, the control of US nuclear missiles can be transferred to the Airborne

Emergency Action Officer on a Looking Glass aircraft with the authority to initiate a second strike.

Since 1990, a Looking Glass plane has been continuously airborne only during times of crisis, such as 9/11. In addition, we now have the Worldwide Airborne Command Post (WWABNCP), a fleet of planes that, once launched, establishes an alternative communications network for US military leaders. Unlike the Soviets, the United States has fully disclosed the existence of Looking Glass and WWABNCP to the world from the start.

What was not known to our enemies at the time was that Presidents Eisenhower, Kennedy, and Johnson had delegated authority to US military commanders in Europe and Asia to launch a nuclear attack if communications were cut off from Washington.[47] The four-star generals who held this authority in turn delegated it to their subordinates in the event they were unreachable.[48] As a result, during the 1950s and 1960s, a large number of overseas US military commanders had the authority to start World War III.[49] The United States also maintained Alternate Joint Communications Centers under Raven Rock Mountain in Pennsylvania and Cheyenne Mountain in Colorado with generals authorized to launch a counterattack if the national political leadership was wiped out by a first strike on Washington, DC.

Kahn understood the importance of convincing the enemy of our capability and resolve to strike back. But he also realized that a SIOP with only one option—a full-scale strike—was not the optimal strategy for conducting a nuclear war. The United States would have no chance to play TFT if the country's next move ended the game forever.

Kahn once recommended to a group of Air Force officers:

> *You make the SAC commander's job hereditary*
> *and put a guy like, say, General LeMay in charge*

who is really going to hit them hard, you know,
and he is really irrevocable. You make his assis-
tant's job to shoot LeMay at the time of war.[50]

Second Strike: Justice or Unjustified?

Like Kahn, I think MAD is based on flawed logic. Kahn's example of General LeMay and his homicidal assistant demonstrates this point.

MAD assumes a first strike by the attacking nation will automatically be followed by a second strike from the defending nation, annihilating the attacking country. Of course, the leaders of any nation must publicly vow to retaliate against a first strike for deterrence to be effective. However, once a full-scale first strike is launched, should the defending nation respond? Regardless of what happens next, most of the citizens in the defending nation are going to die. But rationally, the leaders of the defending nation should consider only the consequences of their actions going forward. A second strike will not bring back their deceased constituents. From the perspective of all humans, not just those in the defending nation, killing hundreds of millions of the attacker's citizens in a second strike now serves no purpose. MAD has failed. The mass murder of hundreds of millions in the defending nation is horrifying and unconscionable. But once a first strike is launched, the soon-to-be dead in the defending country are a sunk cost.

Some believe that retribution is more important than the utilitarian argument that launching a second strike kills hundreds of millions more people without an offsetting benefit. The argument is that a second strike is a righteous response, an eye-for-an-eye Old Testament form of justice. However, it is highly unlikely that hundreds of millions of the soon-to-be incinerated innocent men, women, and children of the attacking country were in favor of a nuclear war. Nations do not hold referendums on first strikes.

Therefore, I think it is amoral to kill hundreds of millions of people in the attacking country because a few of their political or military leaders went crazy. When the time comes, political leaders in the defending nation may reason similarly.

But this contradicts one of the basic assumptions of MAD: that a second strike will follow the first as certain as night follows day. Without this, the logic of MAD falls apart.

Second Strike: Turning a Nuclear Autumn into Winter

MAD is further undermined by the impact of nuclear war on the global climate. This phenomenon was not well understood at the time Kahn wrote *OTW*.

Atomic bombs are different from other weapons. After the initial explosion, there is an aftershock that levels structures around ground zero, piling up kindling that combusts to feed firestorms. The smoke from these firestorms billows into the skies, and the resulting soot hangs in the atmosphere, blotting out the sun's rays and cooling the planet.

The extent of a nuclear winter depends on the number of bombs exploded. An exchange of the entire US and Russian nuclear arsenals of more than eleven thousand warheads would send an estimated 150 million tons of soot into the skies, dropping global temperatures by 15 to 25 degrees Celsius for years, cutting growing seasons by 90 percent, and leading to the death of almost the entire human race from starvation.[51] On the other hand, the detonation of two atomic bombs over Japan in 1945 had no measurable impact on the global climate. In between these two extremes, there are varying degrees of global cooling from a nuclear war.

The extent of the cooling depends on numerous factors:

- The amount of soot generated from fires on the ground after the explosion: Cities have much higher fuel loads and combustibles that burn for longer and at higher temperatures. Hence, detonations over densely built-up urban areas will generate more soot than those over unpopulated rural areas.

- The amount of soot that billows into the upper troposphere: This will depend on winds, precipitation levels, temperature inversions, and other weather conditions. But at higher altitudes, the sun's rays heat the soot, lifting it into the stratosphere where there is no rain to wash it out.

- The amount of sunlight the soot particles absorb once airborne: Soot particles mix with other nonabsorptive aerosols, become coated with other materials that do not retain sunlight, or coagulate with other light-absorbing materials.[52]

The threshold for a worldwide catastrophe is difficult to determine. In 1997, the director of the Central Intelligence Agency estimated it would take the detonation of several hundred average-sized bombs.[53] A 2007 study stated that one hundred bombs would be sufficient.[54] A 2010 research report claimed "a few hundred" would be necessary.[55] A more recent 2020 research report coauthored by nineteen scientists in five countries concluded that even a limited war between Pakistan and India involving strikes from fifty missiles (twenty-five from each arsenal) would result in "the largest famine in documented history."[56]

Of course, modeling the global climate through computer simulations is not an exact science. We struggle to predict whether it will rain tomorrow. And the outputs of the models are only as good as the inputs, which can vary widely, such as weather conditions at the time or the number of detonations over urban areas. But the downside from a nuclear winter is severe enough that we should err on the side of caution.

Let's assume that a nuclear war will target mostly urban areas, most of the soot will make it into the stratosphere, and most of that soot will coagulate with other light-absorbing materials. Based on the above, the research indicates that a nuclear war involving more than two hundred nuclear bombs would result in a nuclear winter that could kill billions.[57]

Given these assumptions, a second strike following a full-scale first strike of thousands of missiles will not have a meaningful impact on the survival rates for residents of the defending or attacking nation: most creatures on Earth will starve to death in the coming months anyway. Even if the first strike were limited to 100 to 150 missiles, a second strike of comparable size would trigger a nuclear winter, increasing the suffering of the citizens of the defending country and people all over the world. The deaths from the first strike, whether from the initial explosions, radioactive fallout, or subsequent global cooling, are sunk costs. The defending nation is only adding to the pile of dead bodies by launching a second strike.

Whether or not you believe in the "justice" of a second strike, the actions of the defending nation will have lethal global consequences. The defending nation could launch a debilitating second strike, annihilating the attacking country and its leadership. In this case, the defending nation would emerge victorious. But this "victory" would plunge the defending country and the world into a nuclear winter and kill billions more.

Those who survive a series of first and second strikes may wish they had not. As President Eisenhower stated, "The only thing worse than losing a global [nuclear] war is winning one."[58]

Although he was not aware of the impact of nuclear war on the global climate, Kahn spent many years thinking deeply about these issues. In the end, he came up with a logical framework that is still used by military strategists today. Based on this framework, Kahn concluded that the United States needed thousands of nuclear weapons.

However, during the 1950s, the world was unaware of the risks of a nuclear winter. Once we input this new data into Kahn's model, the conclusions are quite different.

Three Types of Deterrence

In his original 1960 paper, "The Nature and Feasibility of War and Deterrence," Kahn specified three types of deterrence.

Type 1 deters a direct attack on the US homeland. Kahn argued that the degree of Type 1 deterrence depends on the capability and willingness of the United States to respond to a first strike. In this case, Russia is making the initial calculation to determine whether a nuclear war is "winnable." In a rational world, Russia will launch a first strike on the US homeland only if it believes the United States is unable or unwilling to respond with a second strike.

Type 2 deters actions other than a direct attack on the US homeland that justify a first strike on the Russian homeland. An example is a Russian attack (conventional or nuclear) on a Western European ally. In this case, the United States is calculating whether a nuclear war is "winnable" in deciding whether to retaliate with nuclear weapons.

Type 3 deters actions other than a direct attack for which the response is something other than a first strike. An example is a Russian invasion of an unallied nation. Type 3 responses could be cutting off diplomatic relations, economic sanctions, or a conventional war through proxies.

In terms of Type 1 deterrence, Kahn argued that "we simply

cannot face the possibility of failure."[59] He viewed a sufficient degree of Type 1 deterrence as an absolute requirement for the survival of the nation.

In terms of Type 2 deterrence, Kahn was less certain. He wrote:

> *Suppose, for example, they have dropped bombs on London, Berlin, Rome, Paris and Bonn but have made no detectable preparation for attacking the United States. . . . If 177 million dead is too high a price to pay for punishing the Soviets for their original aggression, how many American dead would we accept as the cost of our retaliation?*[60]

Kahn understood that a first strike by the United States in response to an invasion of Europe would likely be met with a second strike by the Russians. Kahn was asking the key question about Type 2 deterrence: How many dead Americans is a free Europe worth? He then goes on to answer his own question:

> *I have discussed this question with many Americans, and after about 15 minutes of discussion their estimates of an acceptable price generally fall between 10 and 60 million dead. . . . No American I have spoken to who was at all serious about the matter believed that US retaliation would be justified—no matter what our commitments were—if more than half our population would be killed.*[61]

Kahn believed Type 2 deterrence involved a calculation of the risks and rewards of responding to provocation by our enemies. Kahn was arguing that, unlike Type 1, there are no bright lines in Type 2 deterrence. This was extremely controversial. As discussed above, the US SIOP at the time called for a massive first strike in response to any number of provocations by the Soviets, many not involving nuclear weapons.

In terms of Type 3 deterrence, Kahn thought the same risk and reward trade-offs applied as in Type 2. However, calculations about Type 3 deterrence did not involve mass casualties among the civilian populations of either the defending or attacking nation. Hence, decisions about Type 3 deterrence were less controversial. He cites the example of the military expenditures for the Korean War after Chinese-backed forces invaded from the North:

> *In June 1950, the United States was engaged in a great debate on whether the defense budget should be 14, 15, or 16 billion dollars. Along came Korea. Congress quickly authorized 60 billion dollars, an increase by a factor of four.*[62]

Nevertheless, Kahn was skeptical about the sustained effectiveness of Type 2 and Type 3 deterrence. He wrote, "The whole history of the 1933–1939 period is a clear example of the failure of Type 2 and Type 3 deterrence."[63] After the publication of *OTW*, Kahn was assailed in the press by those on the left, who thought he was a warmonger, and many on the right, who accused him of being soft on communism.

Deterrence and the Size of the US Nuclear Arsenal

The logical framework laid out by Kahn more than seventy years ago still holds today. This is a testament to Kahn's brilliance as a strategic thinker.

During his lifetime, Kahn believed that the United States should maintain stockpiles of thousands of nuclear weapons to retain the capability to escalate all the way up his forty-four-rung ladder.[64] But there has been a fundamental change since his death in 1983 in the willingness of Americans to die in a war with the Russians or Chinese. In addition, Kahn did not know about the devastating impact of a nuclear war on the global climate. Given these two new facts, if Kahn were alive today, I believe he would reduce his estimates of the number of warheads that should be held by the United States from thousands to hundreds.

Type 1 Deterrence:
Full-Scale First Strike by Russia

In the case of a full-scale first strike against the United States involving thousands of warheads, a large portion of the population would die, some from the blast and radioactive fallout but most from starvation over the following months. Earth would be plunged into a nuclear winter in which billions would die from a worldwide famine.

At this point, the number of nuclear warheads in the US stockpile would not really matter. Sure, we could annihilate Russia, the only country today and for the foreseeable future that has enough missiles and atomic bombs to launch a full-scale first strike. However, most Russians (and Americans) would soon die from lack of food anyway. A full-scale first strike would be basically suicidal for the Russians, even without an American response. When someone plans to commit suicide, threatening to kill them is not an effective deterrent.

Furthermore, a second strike would only make a nuclear winter longer and more severe, threatening the lives of those Americans who survived a first strike. A second strike would also imperil the lives of billions of people around the world. Many of those who are not residents of the United States and Russia would die from starvation through absolutely no fault of their own.[65]

Therefore, I do not see the justification for a second strike after a full-scale first strike. A second strike will not bring back the American dead and could kill many more, including Americans still alive. In this case, there is no need to deploy thousands of nuclear warheads to guarantee the survival of enough missiles to launch a second strike. After a full-scale first strike on the United States, there is no need for nuclear weapons at all.

Type 1 Deterrence: Limited First Strike by Russia

In the case of a limited first strike against the United States, the analysis is more complex. Assume a first strike of fifty warheads. A full-scale second strike could knock out the remaining thousands of Russian missiles and limit further strikes. However, a full-scale second strike would also plunge the planet into a global winter—suicide for both countries.

The United States could respond with a second strike of comparable magnitude. If reason prevails, then the fighting should end there. But deploying thousands of nuclear warheads is not necessary for a limited second strike: a stockpile of two hundred warheads would be more than enough to sustain a first strike of fifty warheads and respond in kind.

But assume reason does not prevail and the fighting escalates. Once the exchange of nuclear weapons exceeds more than two hundred detonations, there is a significant risk of a global nuclear winter. At that point, further strikes will likely only worsen outcomes for the United States and Russia. Beyond the threshold of nuclear winter, the warring parties are also inflicting suffering on billions of noncombatants. It would not be rational or moral to continue to fight once the threshold of nuclear winter was crossed. Assume the ratio of warheads launched to destroyed is one to one and the threshold of a global nuclear winter is two hundred detonations. In this simple example, a stockpile of no more than two hundred weapons is required (one hundred destroyed by enemy missiles, leaving one hundred for counterattacks).

Type 2 Deterrence: Limited First Strike by the United States

In the case of the United States launching a limited first strike against a foreign nation for invading one of our allies, many have argued that an arsenal of thousands of nuclear warheads would be important. (I have excluded the scenario of a full-scale first strike, as I do not believe the United States would plunge the planet into a nuclear winter to defend an ally.) To discourage a counterattack, many believe that the United States would want to convince the defending country that a second strike was futile. This means demonstrating that thousands of nuclear warheads are at the ready.

But I do not believe America today or in the future will use nuclear weapons for Type 2 deterrence.

After World War II, in its battle against global communism, the United States made a public commitment to defend the NATO countries, as well as Japan, South Korea, and Taiwan. Part of the reason the United States put this security assurance in place is that stationing US conventional forces in those countries sufficient to repel any attack is prohibitively expensive. Instead, the United States covers those nations with a nuclear umbrella and promises of a nuclear response to an invasion. Because nuclear weapons are a lot less costly than conventional forces stationed overseas, this policy has saved American taxpayers hundreds of billions of dollars over the last seventy years. And the US nuclear umbrella has conserved more than just taxpayer money. Without nuclear weapons, the United States would have had to reinstitute the draft, taking men and women out of the workplace and home for military service overseas. Since the 1970s, no American has been forced to serve, which has been a policy quite popular with sons, daughters, and parents alike. For the United States, nuclear weapons have been a way to purchase defense on the cheap. In the case of Europe, the extension of the American nuclear umbrella over NATO was a means to prevent a superior Soviet army from overwhelming the spent Western European nations and militaries recovering from World War II. (There also may have been other reasons. As Lord Hastings Ismay, the first secretary general of NATO, observed, "The goal of NATO was to keep the Americans in, the Russians out, and the Germans down."[66])

Today, the situation is reversed: most analysts believe the conventional forces of NATO resident in Europe are more than a match for the Russian Army.[67] NATO has superior conventional capabilities in cruise missiles, antiaircraft weapons, gravity bombs, defense interceptors, and short-range ballistic missiles.[68] Soviet leaders seemed to have all but acknowledged this fact in 1993 by withdrawing a no-first-use pledge concerning nuclear weapons in Europe because of doubts about the ability of Soviet forces to withstand a NATO invasion.[69] Furthermore, Russian leaders seem to be much more interested in advancing economically than geographically, with the exception of Ukraine. Extended and costly wars are not good for increasing a country's gross domestic product or maintaining the continued support of the Russian people. See the Russian invasion and subsequent withdrawal from Afghanistan.

In the South China Sea, the situation is different. In 1960, China could not have conquered Taiwan. China at that time was consumed with some domestic matters, such as the Great Leap Forward (1958–1962) and the Cultural Revolution (1966–1976), which combined killed more than forty million people.[70] Chairman Mao was too distracted waging war against his fellow comrades to open up another front on the island of Taiwan with the Republic of China.

Today, the greatly enlarged and increasingly technically sophisticated Chinese Red Army will soon be able to successfully invade Taiwan. In recent years, the rhetoric of senior Chinese leadership concerning Taiwan has become increasingly aggressive. In 2021, China flew a record twenty-eight warplanes into Taiwanese airspace in one sortie to test the nation's air defenses.[71]

Despite the coverage the nuclear umbrella offered to our allies in the past, I question whether US security assurances are still in force. Would a US president today trade Tampa for Taipei? Wichita for Warsaw? In 1960, Kahn's informal survey suggests that tens of millions of Americans were willing to make the ultimate sacrifice and destroy large parts of our country forever to stop the spread of communism and protect our allies overseas. In my view, that is no longer the case.

Fortunately, NATO forces today are stronger than those in Russia, and the former Soviet Union is not hell-bent on overthrowing capitalism. But China's military is more powerful and its leadership more outwardly aggressive than ever before. In the coming decades, Chinese People's Liberation Army tanks could roll over protestors in Liberty Square in Taipei. I do not believe the American people will be willing to die in the tens of millions to stop them.

Thus, we do not require thousands of nuclear weapons to launch first strikes against Russia and China in defense of our allies. In fact, I do not think America would launch a nuclear first strike against any nation other than in response to an attack on the US homeland.

The facts on the ground have changed. The US nuclear umbrella no longer extends as a practical matter over Europe and Asia. Thus, in terms of Type 2 deterrence, there is no role for nuclear weapons at all.

Type 3 Deterrence: No Nukes

Type 3 deterrence is based on the use of conventional weapons and other coercive measures. No need for nuclear weapons here either.

How Much Is Enough: Less Than Before

Based on the above analysis, there is no role for US nuclear weapons in Type 1 full-scale attack and Type 2 deterrence. There is a place for US nuclear weapons in Type 1 limited first strike deterrence, but I have argued that two hundred nuclear warheads should be sufficient to respond to a limited first strike without plunging the world into a nuclear winter. In addition, the world today is a lot different from the world of 1960, when Kahn concluded that thousands of nuclear warheads were required for the US stockpile.

First, the world is now more urbanized. When the Cold War first started, Russia was largely an agrarian nation. Today, about 70 percent of Russians live in urban areas, and that percentage is expected to grow.[72] The top fifteen Russian cities currently house approximately thirty-one million people, or 22 percent of the total population.[73] In China, the percentage of the population that lives in urban areas rose from 19 percent to 63 percent from 1980 to 2020.[74] The top fifteen Chinese cities hold 260 million people, or 20 percent of the total population.[75] Launching strikes on the fifteen largest urban areas in either Russia or China would devastate those nations. Today, we do not have to bomb the whole country, and so we do not need as many bombs.

Second, atomic bombs are bigger. The bombs dropped on Hiroshima ("Little Boy") and Nagasaki ("Fat Man") could level about three square miles. Since then, we have developed thermonuclear devices that can destroy seventy-five square miles.[76] Today, we get more bang per bang.

Third, missiles are more precise. Even during the 1970s, long-range ballistic missiles were not accurate enough to hit most of their targets. But onboard computers now continuously correct the trajectory of a missile in flight. In 1985, one study showed that an ICBM had a 54 percent chance of destroying a hardened target.[77] Today, because of greater accuracy, a bomb of equal size has a 74 percent chance.[78] The increase in accuracy for sea-launched ballistic missiles (SLBMs) over the same period is even greater.[79]

Fourth, fratricide is less of a problem. During the Cold War, we planned to send multiple missiles to each target because some portion of the missiles would miss. But the effects from the detonation of the first warhead, such as radiation and heat, can destroy or deflect the second incoming warhead.[80] The explosion of the first warhead also vaporizes and uplifts debris from the ground. This debris cools within six to eight seconds into solid masses that can be lethal to incoming missiles.[81] Thus, for the second detonation to be effective, it needs to occur five to six seconds after the first bomb. With today's more accurate guidance systems, we can hit a much larger percentage of the targets, reducing the need for a second, third, or even fourth bomb to overcome fratricide.

Fifth, our warheads are less vulnerable. In 1960, most of our warheads were in ground-based silos. Today, submarines carry most of our deployed nuclear weapons. The locations of our ICBM silos and bombers are pretty much known to our enemies. The locations of most of our submarines are not. Some technologies on the horizon, such as low-frequency active and passive sonars, underwater lasers, and autonomous underwater vehicles, could change that. However, for the foreseeable future, our submarines will be nearly impossible for the enemy to target.

I do not know the exact number of nuclear warheads that would be optimal for the United States to deploy today and in the years ahead. But it is certainly less than the 5,550 warheads currently in our nuclear stockpile. And whatever that optimal number is, it is a lot lower than it was in 1960 when Kahn wrote *OTW*.

Spending Money on Weapons We Do Not Need

Our fleet of nuclear weapons and related systems are aging, and many are long past their due dates for replacement or refurbishment. The Congressional Budget Office estimates it will cost $1.2 trillion in current dollars ($1.7 trillion including inflation) between 2016 and 2046 to update our nuclear capabilities.[82] That is in addition to the more than $350 billion we spend each decade maintaining the existing nuclear arsenal.[83]

The United States has roughly 3,570 warheads in the military stockpile and 1,750 awaiting decommissioning.[84] The weapons in the military stockpile are mostly SLBMs, which ride on Trident missiles in submarines lurking beneath ocean waters (1,920); the rest are split about evenly between bombers (850) and ground-based ICBMs (800). The bombers are stationed at various US Air Force bases, and the ICBMs are housed in underground silos in Montana, North Dakota, and Wyoming. About one hundred bombs are in Europe on six bases in five countries. The SLBMs and ICBMs are mostly multiple independently targetable reentry vehicles, but those on bombers and on European bases are not.

A small fraction of the $1.2 trillion budgeted to be spent upgrading US nuclear munitions would be sufficient to decommission most of the 3,570 warheads in the military stockpile today (the 1,750 awaiting retirement will have to be paid for in any case). The rest of the monies could be used to build up our conventional forces over the same period. For example, we could increase our ability to strike at our enemies by arming ICBMs, cruise missiles, and other precision weapons systems that today carry atomic bombs with conventional munitions. In addition, we could invest more in autonomous drones guided by artificial intelligence. Transitioning to a greater reliance on technologically advanced conventional precision weapons need not cost more.

Conclusions

In my judgment, the United States could prudently cut its nuclear stockpile to hundreds of atomic bombs, somewhere between two hundred and one thousand warheads. That is a wide range, but a definite number will require critical pieces of information that today we do not have. Most important, we need to carefully study the impacts of a nuclear war on the global climate. The amount of government funding for research on nuclear winter pales in comparison to the amount spent on nuclear arms. It is critical to know, before the shooting starts, at what point a nuclear autumn turns into a nuclear winter. I have referenced some of the few existing scientific studies. We need a lot more.

Since 1960 the world has changed. We now know the risk of nuclear winter is real. The American public is no longer willing to sacrifice our nation to protect our allies. Our adversaries are more urbanized. Our bombs are bigger and more precise. Our warheads are less vulnerable. Missile fratricide is less of a problem. During the Cold War, in confronting an aggressive, ideologically driven adversary, the United States had good reasons to deploy thousands of nuclear weapons. Today's Russia is more internally focused.

The rationale to significantly cut back our nuclear stockpile goes beyond potential cost savings. If the tripwire for a full-scale second strike is the single use of an atomic weapon, then we are falling back into the insane logic of MAD. In a full-scale nuclear war, victory is an illusion and retribution pointless. Our generation has a historic opportunity to achieve the most significant arms control limitation treaty since atomic bombs were invented, reducing the risk of a global holocaust.

As mentioned earlier, China has about 320 nuclear warheads. The countries with the next largest atomic arsenals are France (290), the United Kingdom (215), Pakistan (160), India (150), Israel (90), and North Korea (30–40).[85]

I do not worry about France, the United Kingdom, or Israel attacking the United States. A US nuclear arsenal of hundreds of bombs is sufficient to launch a devastating second strike on China, Pakistan, India, or North Korea. None of these nations have a full-scale first-strike capability.

So the issue is Russia.

In my view, Russia has more to fear from China than the United States. Reports indicate that China plans to double its nuclear stockpile and that Russia is moving many of its mobile nuclear launch vehicles to eastern Russia to be closer to its Asian neighbor.[86]

The United States should offer to cap the number of warheads in the US nuclear arsenal to a number less than one thousand if China and Russia agree to do the same. The United States does not need thousands of nuclear warheads. Russia should welcome the chance to forestall an arms race with China. And China should prefer parity with Russia and the United States over the status quo.[87]

Even if Russia and China agreed to a proposal to limit the number of nuclear warheads in their respective arsenals to less than one thousand, it would still be a MAD world.

Just a little saner.

Another example of the role of game theory in military strategy is from World War I, fought from 1914 to 1918. Unfortunately, the British commander in chief who sent millions of men "over the top" to be shredded by German artillery and machine guns did not understand much about the subject.

However, he was an excellent horseman and avid polo player. Perhaps that explains his belief that "aeroplanes and tanks are only accessories to the man and the horse."[88]

CHAPTER 6

Wars of Attrition: World War I, Justice, and Relationships

Sir Douglas Haig:
The War to End All Wars and Horses

Sir Douglas Haig (1861–1928) was the chief of staff of the British Expeditionary Force in France and the architect of battlefield strategy for the Allied armies during World War I. Haig was the son of a successful whisky distiller in Scotland and the youngest of eleven children.[1] His father sold the distillery to Distillers Company (later United Distillers) in 1877, which gave the family substantial wealth. (United Distillers was acquired by Diageo Group in 1997, and Haig whisky remains in production today.) He was educated in Scotland but transferred to Oxford when he was eighteen after the death of his parents, his mother from ill health and his father from alcoholism. At Oxford, he excelled at polo and was mostly remembered for his love of horses.

Impatient to make his mark, Haig left Oxford before taking a degree and joined the army. In 1886, the army allowed him to tour the United States as part of the English national polo team. After returning from the United States, the army posted him to India for six years, and subsequently he fought in the Mahdist War in Sudan. Afterward, Haig was sent to South Africa as a major in the Second Boer War and, in 1903, returned to India as inspector-general of the cavalry.

Haig left India in 1911 and when war broke out in 1914 was put in charge of the First and Second Divisions of the British Expeditionary Force. In December 1914, the British military command was reorganized, and Haig was placed in command of the First Army. When Sir John French resigned in late 1915, Haig was promoted to commander in chief of the British forces in France. Haig retired at the conclusion of World War I and worked to establish charities to support wounded ex-servicemen. He died in 1928, aged sixty-six, and was buried in Scotland in a grave marked by a simple, plain stone tablet, identical to one placed over the remains of a common soldier.

Hell Cannot Be So Terrible

World War I was a war of attrition. Each side continued to fight for years and suffered losses far beyond the gains that would come from victory. In the end, the Allied powers won, but it was not worth the cost. The estimated economic losses from the war were $2.7 trillion, or about double the world's 1913 GDP.[2] At least fifteen million soldiers died, and another twenty-three million soldiers were wounded, many disabled for life.[3] For four bloody years, French and German soldiers, along with those from the United Kingdom and twenty-seven other nations, battled to the death in a line of

Oskar Morgenstern (1902–1977) (left) and John von Neumann (1903–1957) on one of their many beach walks in New Jersey, where they discussed their ground-breaking work, *Theory of Games and Economic Behavior*. This work, coauthored in 1944, was the foundational text that established game theory as a formal branch of mathematics. *Photograph by Dorothy Morgenstern Thomas, courtesy of the Morgenstern Estate. From the Shelby White and Leon Levy Archives Center, via the Institute for Advanced Study (Princeton, NJ).*

John Forbes Nash, Jr. (1928–2015) was a Nobel Prize-winning mathematician and economist who is most famous for the Nash equilibrium, which proved that there is an optimal strategy for many types of games, such as the prisoner's dilemma. *Photographer/Artist: South China Morning Post (Getty Images).*

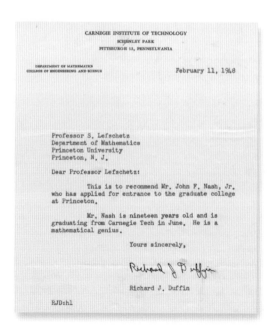

The recommendation letter from Nash's undergraduate advisor at Carnegie Mellon submitted as part of Nash's application to the PhD program at Princeton. This may be the best recommendation letter ever written on a per word basis.

Simple Examples

These are intended to illustrate the concepts defined in the paper and display special phenomena which occur in these games.

The first player has the roman letter strategies and the pay-off to the left, etc.

Ex. 1

$$\begin{array}{rll} 5 & a\alpha & -3 \\ -4 & a\beta & 4 \\ -5 & b\alpha & 5 \\ 5 & b\beta & -4 \end{array}$$

Weak Solution: $\left(\frac{9}{16}a + \frac{7}{16}b, \frac{7}{17}\alpha + \frac{10}{17}\beta\right)$

$V_1 = \frac{-5}{17}$, $V_2 = +\frac{1}{2}$

Ex. 2

$$\begin{array}{rll} 1 & a\alpha & 1 \\ -10 & a\beta & 10 \\ 10 & b\alpha & -10 \\ -1 & b\beta & -1 \end{array}$$

Strong Solution: (b, β)

$V_1 = V_2 = -1$

Ex. 3

$$\begin{array}{rll} 1 & a\alpha & 1 \\ -10 & a\beta & -10 \\ -10 & b\alpha & -10 \\ 1 & b\beta & 1 \end{array}$$

Unsolvable; equilibrium points $(a\alpha)$, (b,β), and $\left(\frac{a}{2} + \frac{b}{2}, \frac{\alpha}{2} + \frac{\beta}{2}\right)$. The strategies in the last case have maxi-min and mini-max properties.

Ex. 4

$$\begin{array}{rll} 1 & a\alpha & 1 \\ 0 & a\beta & 1 \\ 1 & b\alpha & 0 \\ 0 & b\beta & 0 \end{array}$$

Strong Solution: all pairs of mixed strategies.

$V_1^+ = V_2^+ = 1$, $V_1^- = V_2^- = 0$

Ex. 5

$$\begin{array}{rll} 1 & a\alpha & 2 \\ -1 & a\beta & -4 \\ -4 & b\alpha & -1 \\ 2 & b\beta & 1 \end{array}$$

Unsolvable; eq. pts. $(a\alpha)$, (b,β) and $\left(\frac{1}{4}a + \frac{3}{4}b, \frac{3}{8}\alpha + \frac{5}{8}\beta\right)$. However, empirical tests show a tendency toward $(a\alpha)$.

Ex. 6

$$\begin{array}{rll} 1 & a\alpha & 1 \\ 0 & a\beta & 0 \\ 0 & b\alpha & 0 \\ 0 & b\beta & 0 \end{array}$$

Eq. pts.: $(a\alpha)$ and (b,β), with (b,β) an example of instability.

John Nash's original 1949 PhD thesis, titled *Non-Cooperative Games*, p. 12a. Nash presents in Ex. 2 the pay-offs for the prisoner's dilemma and labels the equivalent of both sides defecting as a "strong solution." His fellow RAND researchers would later show that this is only true for a game of prisoner's dilemma played once. *Photo courtesy of the RAND Corporation. https://www.rand.org/about/history/a-brief-history-of-rand.html*

The original RAND building at 1700 Main Street in Santa Monica, California, where Tucker spotted Nash's Ex. 2 on a blackboard. Incorporated as a non-profit on May 14, 1948, RAND employed John von Neumann, John Nash, Herman Kahn, and others to formulate military strategy for the US Air Force. *Photo © and courtesy of the RAND Corporation. https://www.rand.org/about/history/a-brief-history-of-rand.html*

RAND strategists in the midst of a 1966 Engineering Operations exercise in which game theory was employed to develop strategies to fight a nuclear war with the Soviet Union. *Photo © and courtesy of the RAND Corporation. https://www.rand.org/about/history/a-brief-history-of-rand.html*

Appendix

Running Comments*

I. Subject AA

Play No.	Comment
1	JW will play 1—sure win. Hence if I play 1—I lose.
2	What is he doing?!!
3	Trying mixed?
4	Has he settled on 1?
5	Perverse!
6	I'm sticking to 2 since he will mix for at least 4 more times.
9	If I mix occasionally, he will switch—but why will he ever switch from 1.
10	Prediction. He will stick with 1 until I change from 2. I feel like DuPont.
19	I'm completely confused. Is he trying to convey information to me?
28	He wants more 1's by me than I'm giving.
31	Some start.
32 - 40	JW is bent on sticking to 1. He will not share at all as a price of getting me to stick to 1.
49	He will not share.
58	He will not share.
59	He does not want to trick me. He is satisfied. I must teach him to share.
67	He won't share.
68	He'll punish for trying!

* The two subjects are friends.

The Appendix from RAND Research Memorandum (RM-789-1) that relates the running comments from Armen Alchian (AA) and John Williams (JW), the two researchers Flood and Dresher enlisted to play the first known experimental test of the prisoner's dilemma. Note how each player alternatively "punishes" and "shares" to determine the willingness of the other player to cooperate. *Photo courtesy of the RAND Corporation. https://www.rand.org/pubs/research_memoranda/RM789-1.html*

Albert Tucker (1905–1995) was a mathematics professor at Princeton who, while visiting a friend in 1950 at RAND Corp., recognized on a blackboard Ex. 2 from John Nash's recently completed PhD thesis. He recast Nash's Ex. 2 in the form of a story about two prisoners. *Office of Communications Records, AC168, Princeton University Archives, Department of Special Collections, Princeton University Library.*

On Jargon
The Prisoner's
Dilemma

A TWO-PERSON DILEMMA

Two men, charged with a joint violation of law, are held separately by the police. Each is told that

(1) if one confesses and the other does not, the former will be given a reward of one unit and the latter will be fined two units,

(2) if both confess, each will be fined one unit.

At the same time each has good reason to believe that

(3) if neither confesses, both will go clear.

This situation gives rise to a simple symmetric two-person game (not zero-sum) with the following table of payoffs, in which each ordered pair represents the payoffs to I and II, in that order:

		II	
		confess	not confess
I	confess	(-1, -1)	(1, -2)
	not confess	(-2, 1)	(0, 0)

Clearly, for each man the pure strategy "confess" dominates the pure strategy "not confess." Hence, there is a unique equilibrium point* given by the two pure strategies "confess." In contrast with this non-cooperative solution one sees that both men would profit if they could form a coalition binding each other to "not confess."

The game becomes zero-sum three-person by introducing the State as a third player. The State exercises no choice (that is, has a single pure strategy) but receives payoffs as follows:

		II	
		confess	not confess
I	confess	2	1
	not confess	1	0

*see J. Nash, PROC. NAT. ACAD. SCI. 36 (1950) 48-49.

Stanford, May 1950   A.W. Tucker

The handout given to Stanford students by Tucker in May 1950 that explains Nash's Ex. 2 in terms of two prisoners deciding whether to confess and provides the basis for what has become known as the prisoner's dilemma. Note that Tucker references Nash at the bottom of the page.

Anatol Rapoport (1911–2007) was a mathematical biologist and psychologist who formulated the Tit-for-Tat strategy that repeatedly won computer simulations of the prisoner's dilemma. He led numerous protest movements and dedicated most of his life to the study of peace. *Photograph courtesy of The Rapoport Family.*

Rapoport was also a world-class pianist, performing with orchestras throughout Europe and the United States. This image is from a recital he gave at the University of Michigan on April 12, 1970. *Photograph courtesy of The Rapoport Family.*

Robert Axelrod (b. 1943) is a political scientist at the University of Michigan and a National Medal of Science winner who conducted a series of computer simulations of the prisoner's dilemma in which the program Tit for Tat, submitted by Anatol Rapoport, was victorious. Axelrod (far right) is working with his colleagues on setting up one of these simulations. *Gerald R. Ford School of Public Policy/University of Michigan.*

Prisoner's Dilemma

If you're looking for a challenge for your strategic instincts and programming skills, the tournament for the Prisoner's Dilemma may be for you.

This national computer tournament is based on a nifty little game called the Prisoner's Dilemma. There are two players, but unlike most games, the players are not in total conflict. In fact, both can do well or both can do poorly.

The game will be played for an average of 200 moves, and in each move, each player can choose either to cooperate or to defect. If both cooperate, both do well. But if one defects while the other cooperates, the defecting player gets his highest payoff, and the cooperating player gets taken for a sucker and gets his lowest payoff. The catch is that if both defect, both do poorly.

Payoffs in the tournament for a given move are 3 points each if both cooperate; 5 points to a player who defects while the other cooperates, with 0 points to the sucker; and 1 point each if they both defect. The score of a player in a single game is his or her total over all moves.

To win the tournament you have to get the highest total score summed over all the games you play. Therefore your object is to get a good score in each separate game, but not necessarily to get a better score than the player with whom you are currently playing.

To join the computer tournament, submit a program written in BASIC or FORTRAN IV which will be a decision rule — a strategy — for selecting the "cooperate" or "defect" choice at each move. The decision rule may be based on the history of the game so far. For example, a simple and effective decision rule is "Tit for Tat": cooperate on the first move, and then do exactly what the other player did on the previous move. Quite sophisticated decision rules can be written in as little as 25 lines.

This tournament for which there is no entrance fee, is part of a research project to understand the nature of skillful performance in a two-sided environment which is partially cooperative and partially competitive.

Each person who completes an entry will receive a report describing the results of the tournament. The winner will receive a report describing the results of the tournament. The winner will receive an engraved trophy.

For more details write to Professor Robert Axelrod, Institute of Public Policy Studies, The University of Michigan, 506 E. Liberty St., Ann Arbor, MI 48104.

The advertisement Axelrod ran in *Personal Computing* magazine to recruit players for the second of his computer tournaments. Note that Axelrod calls out Tit for Tat as a strategy after its success in the first tournament and offers the winner "an engraved trophy." *Photo from* Personal Computing *magazine.*

John Maynard Smith (1920–2004) was a mathematical biologist who developed the concept of an evolutionary stable strategy (ESS) that explains much about animal and human behavior, particularly the "battle between the sexes." *Andrew Hasson/Alamy Stock Photo.*

Herman Kahn (1922–1983) was the founder of the Hudson Institute and the author of *On Thermonuclear War*, which one reviewer called "pornography for officers." His lectures could be six hours long, given without notes, and accompanied by hundreds of charts and graphs. *Photo by Jerome Liebling/Getty Images.*

Douglas Haig (1861–1928) was the British military leader during World War I who was nicknamed "Butcher Haig" for the two million British casualties suffered under his command. Years later in 1926, Haig predicted that "as time goes on you find just as much use for the horse—the well-bred horse—as you have ever done in the past . . . aeroplanes and tanks are only accessories . . ." Haig was an avid polo player. *Photographer/Artist: W. and D. Downey (Getty Images).*

The Battle of the Somme was fought from July to November 1916. British forces under the command of Douglas Haig incurred over 400,000 casualties. Haig's report back to London in the midst of the Battle of the Somme was upbeat and concluded, "The picture is full of encouragement and promise." *Photographer/Artist: PA Images (Getty Images).*

Charles Dodgson (aka Lewis Carroll) (1832–1898) was a brilliant mathematician and author of *Alice's Adventures in Wonderland*. Among his many achievements was the development of one of the first versions of ranked-choice voting, known today as the Dodgson method. *Ian Dagnall Computing /Alamy Stock Photo.*

Kenneth Arrow (1921–2017) was a Nobel Prize-winning economist who proved the impossibility of constructing an optimal election system, or what is known as the Arrow Impossibility Theorem. Arrow stated, "Most systems are not going to work badly all the time. All I proved is that all can work badly at times." *Keystone Press/Alamy Stock Photo.*

William Vickrey (1914–1996) was a Nobel Prizing-winning economist who advocated the use of sealed-bid second-price auctions, which later became known as Vickrey auctions. Decades later, Vickrey auctions would become the most widely used mechanism for price discovery in the online world. *Richard Drew/AP/Shutterstock.*

trenches that stretched from the icy waters of the English Channel to the snowy mountains of Switzerland.

A French lieutenant who fought and was later killed at Verdun wrote in his diary: "Humanity is mad. It must be mad to do what it is doing. What a massacre! Hell cannot be so terrible."[4]

A German soldier expressed similar thoughts: "The war would not be over until the last German and the last French hobble out of the trenches to exterminate each other with pocketknives."[5]

The Battle of the Somme was particularly bloody. At 7:30 a.m. on July 1, 1916, the barrage of artillery fire that had been pounding the German lines for seven days fell silent. British infantry units emerged from the trenches along sixteen miles of the front into bright sunshine and advanced, shoulder to shoulder, across no-man's-land, to be cut down by German guns and artillery in a hail of bullets and shells. By the end of that day, Haig had sent 110,000 infantrymen over the top. Nearly twenty thousand were killed, and another forty thousand were wounded.[6] The official history of the British Army records that "the extended lines started in excellent order, but gradually melted away. There was no wavering or attempting to come back, the men fell in their ranks, mostly before the first hundred yards of No Man's Land had been crossed."[7]

Yet Haig's account of the Battle of the Somme at the time was upbeat. His report back to London read: "The picture is full of encouragement and promise. . . . The German soldiers are now practically beaten and ready to surrender . . . thoroughly tired of the war and hopeless of eventual success."[8] The Battle of the Somme would continue for several more months at the cost of more than four hundred thousand British casualties.

Haig defended his decisions at the Battle of the Somme to the end of his life. He claimed the lesson learned from World War I was that the Allied powers did not have sufficient men and materials to break through the German lines. Haig was particularly concerned, perhaps based on his Oxford polo days, that there would be enough horses to fight the next war. In 1926, he alluded to this in a speech:

> *I believe that the value of a horse and the opportunity of the horse in the future is likely to be as great as ever. Aeroplanes and tanks are only accessories to the man and the horse, and I feel sure that as time goes on you will find just as much use for the horse—the well-bred horse—as you have ever done in the past.*[9]

Besides his misconceptions about modern warfare, Haig did not understand the nature of wars of attrition. Under Haig's command, more than two million British soldiers were killed or wounded by the end of the Great War, a loss in human lives that far exceeded the gains from victory.

Overpaying: The Rational Choice

In wars of attrition, combatants on both sides are typically worse off by the end of the battle. In fact, this seemingly irrational behavior by both parties—continuing to fight beyond the point at which the costs of battle exceed the gains from victory—is predicted by game theory. This is because wars of attrition are equivalent to an all-pay auction, in which each player bids on an item but, unlike a regular auction, losers must pay their last bid.

Assume an item in an all-pay auction is worth $100. Sally and Mary compete for the item, and after several rounds of bidding Sally has bid $100, topping Mary's previous $90 bid. If Mary stops bidding, then Sally will win the auction and Mary will be out $90. So Mary reasons that if she bids $110 and wins, she will still be better off than if she had not bid again, even though the item is worth only $100. Mary is already out $90, her last bid. But by bidding $110, or $20 more, she has the chance to gain the $100 prize. If she wins, then she will have an incremental gain of $80 ($100 – $20). If she stops bidding, then she will have no gain or loss, since her previous bid of $90 is a sunk cost. Once Mary bids $110, then Sally should make a similar calculation. If Sally bids $120, she will also gain $80 ($100 – $20). If Sally does not bid, then there is no gain or loss, because her last bid of $100 is also a sunk cost.

If the value of the item is worth more than the incremental bid amount, then the rational strategy is to keep bidding. In all-pay auctions, once the bidding starts, the bidders will continue to escalate their offers, even submitting bids that exceed the value of the item at auction, until the other bidders have run out of money. While Sally and Mary did not make a bad decision along the way, they ended up with a ruinous outcome. One of the two will overpay for the item, and the other will pay for an item she does not get.

For bidders in an all-pay auction, the key determination is how much money the other bidders have. If the other bidders have more money than you do, then you should never participate in an all-pay auction. If the amount of money you have exceeds that of the other bidders, and the amount of money the other bidders have is less than the value of the item at auction, then you should participate. If all bidders are rational and have complete information, the bidder with the most money should be the only person to participate in the auction.

A Ruinous Outcome Predicted by Game Theory

World War I was, in effect, an all-pay auction: the bids were losses of men and materials and the item at auction was victory in Europe. In this horrific real-life all-pay auction, each battle was the equivalent of a bidding round with both sides paying the price in men and materials regardless of whether they won that round. In the end, both the victorious Allies and the defeated Central powers paid the cost of their final bid, the sum of all the losses incurred over the course of the Great War, almost forty million dead and wounded and twice the GDP of the entire world.

Both sides believed they had more resources, measured in men and materials, than the other side and hence could outlast their enemy and gain the prize of victory in Europe. Haig's belief was correct that if the Allies were willing to sacrifice the lives of tens of millions of their own, then the Central powers would eventually stop fighting, unwilling to kill more of their own citizens, the equivalent of running out of money in an all-pay auction. But Haig failed to understand that wars of attrition are like all-pay auctions in which the losses from battle often exceed the gains from victory. Given the potential for a ruinous outcome, the Allied and Central powers nations should have avoided the war. The nations of Europe would have been better off negotiating a settlement rather than fighting.

To illustrate, suppose the values of two nations, one warlike and one peaceful, are equal to $100, the cost of a battle is $20 per side, and the odds of winning a war are fifty-fifty.

Imagine the warlike nation threatens war. If the peaceful nation fights and wins, it will gain the $100 prewar value of the other nation, less the $20 each side spent fighting, for a total of $60. If the peaceful nation fights and loses, it will lose $100, the prewar value of the country. The odds of winning are 50 percent. Therefore, for the peaceful nation, the expected value of fighting is the average of a positive $60 and a negative $100, or a negative $20. Hence, the peaceful nation should be willing to give the warlike nation something less than $20 not to attack. Of course, the peaceful nation will agree to pay only if this is the last of the warlike nation's extortionary demands. Otherwise, the warlike nation will just continue to threaten until there is nothing left for the peaceful nation to give.

But no entity in history has been able to guarantee the enforcement of international agreements between nations. Thus, there is no effective way for the peaceful nation to enforce a bargain with the warlike nation, after the first payment is made by the peaceful country.

Note that for the warlike nation the expected value from fighting a war is also a negative $20. In our example, the costs and payoffs are symmetrical. If the peaceful country makes clear it will always fight back, then the warlike nation would be better off not attacking. At the same time, the peaceful country also expects to lose $20 if it fights back every time. Ideally, the peaceful country would like to convince the warlike nation it will fight, even if that is not true.

Mixed Strategies: Pretending to Be What You Are Not

In game theory, adopting the same strategy consistently is known as a pure strategy. Alternating strategies, the approach recommended by Sun Tzu in *The Art of War* from Chapter 1, is called a mixed strategy. A mixed strategy randomly switches between strategies to confuse an opponent, or what Sun Tzu called responding in an "infinite variety of ways."

In many games and in real life, we should play a mixed strategy to prevent others from extorting us. If the peaceful nation always surrenders, then the warlike nation will constantly threaten war to extract a payment. If the peaceful nation always fights, then it can expect to experience a net loss of $20 on average. However, if the peaceful nation adopts a mixed strategy, alternating between fighting and surrendering, then it should be able to deter the warlike nation from attacking. Recall that the payoffs from fighting are symmetrical: the warlike nation also incurs an expected loss of $20 from fighting. Hence, the warlike nation will threaten to attack only if it believes some portion of the time that the peaceful nation will surrender.

But how often should the peaceful nation fight back to deter the warlike nation from threatening war?

The answer depends on the value of the prize, the cost of the fighting, and the probability the opponent will surrender.

Assume as before that if the warlike nation attacks and the peaceful nation fights back and wins, then the warlike nation loses $100, the value of its nation. If the warlike nation wins, then the warlike nation gains the value of the peaceful nation after the war ($100 – $20) less the costs of battle to the warlike nation ($20), or $60. Because the odds of winning are fifty-fifty, the expected value for the warlike nation when the peaceful nation fights is the average of losing $100 and gaining $60, or a negative $20. If the peaceful nation immediately surrenders, the warlike nation gains $100, the value of the peaceful nation.

Based on these assumptions, the peaceful nation should fight back five out of six times to incentivize the warlike nation not to attack. If the peaceful nation fights back five out of six times, then the expected value for the warlike nation from attacking the peaceful nation is zero, or ($20 loss × ⅚) + ($100 gain × ⅙). The same expected value calculation applies to the peaceful nation, so the threat to fight back five out of six times is credible.

If the peaceful nation fights back more than five out of every six times, then the expected payoff to the warlike nation is negative. If the peaceful nation fights back less than that amount, then the payoff is positive. But the peaceful nation wants to fight back the minimal number of times necessary to prevent exploitation, since the expected value from a war is negative. Therefore, the optimal mixed strategy for the peaceful nation is to fight five out of six times.

The peaceful nation's optimal mixed strategy depends on the relative value of the two nations, the costs of battle, and the odds of victory. The more valuable the peaceful country and thus the higher the expected value for the warlike country from winning, the more often the peaceful nation should fight back to deter aggression. That means that larger and wealthier nations should fight back more often, as they have more to lose. The greater the cost of battle, the less often the peaceful nation should fight back, as the expected losses from fighting are greater. An important determinant of the cost of battle is how long a nation is willing to fight. Thus, nations publicly vow to "fight on to the death" to raise the costs of battle. The greater the odds of victory for the peaceful nation, the more often the peaceful nation should fight back, as the expected value from war is less for the warlike nation. Hence, more powerful peaceful countries should be more willing to enter into battle.

To avoid wars of attrition, whether between nations or individuals, players should adopt mixed strategies to deter other players from fighting. After repeated interactions, players should see that there are no gains from fighting with those that have adopted optimal mixed strategies. By contrast, players that pursue pure strategies offer an incentive for the other side to call their bluff and to threaten war. Both sides benefit when the peaceful player adopts an optimal mixed strategy.

Mixed strategies are quite common, even among the youngest members of society. Think rock-paper-scissors. Nations, companies, and individuals regularly employ mixed strategies in the equivalent of all-pay auctions to discourage others from attacking.

An example is the administration of justice.

Justice Systems: The State Has the Most Force

Imagine a community comprising one warlike individual and many peaceful individuals but without a system of justice. In other words, no police, judges, or jails. Also, suppose the cost and payoffs from attacking another individual are the same as in the case of the warlike and peaceful nations above. If a peaceful person is attacked and loses, then the warlike person takes the peaceful person's property valued at $100. If the peaceful person wins, then they gain the $100 of property owned by the warlike person. In either case, the peaceful and warlike individuals both sustain $20 in the form of injuries. By the same logic as before, the optimal mixed strategy is for a peaceful individual to fight back five out of six times.

But fighting hurts overall welfare, as the property fought over was already owned by the members of the community. Fighting produces no net gain, only a reallocation between individuals. Regardless of who wins, the overall welfare of the group is reduced by the amount of the costs of fighting.

By establishing a strong central authority, in the form of police, judges, and jails, fighting between individuals can be discouraged. A strong central authority acts like a peaceful individual who, when attacked, always wins. In this scenario, the calculus for the warlike individual changes. The expected value from fighting for the warlike individual is always a negative $100, and thus it never makes sense to attack.

The overwhelming force of a strong central authority is analogous to the bidder in an all-pay auction who clearly has more money than everyone else. If that bidder has demonstrably more funds than the others, then no other bidders should place an initial bid. Similarly, within a community, if a central authority has an overwhelming capability for violence, far in excess of any individual community member or groups of individuals, then an aggressive act by one individual against another will result in the defeat of the attacker by the central authority. Hence, it is irrational for an attacker to strike another member of the community.

Another advantage of a strong central authority to mete out retribution is that the punishment can be independent of the attacker and the defender. Without a strong central authority, the response to an act of aggression would depend on the relative strengths of the combatants: stronger members of a community would be able to literally get away with murder. With a strong central authority, the weak and the strong are more equally protected. This more equal treatment of all within a community creates a sense of justice. With a strong central authority, might no longer means right. I suspect that among the first laws established by central authorities were rules for punishing violent behavior, independent of the parties involved. (This also explains one of the practical benefits of religion. The promise of punishments and rewards from a powerful divine being who sees all is an example of an overwhelming powerful central authority that can discourage acts of aggression. In addition, God is an unbiased third-party arbiter of justice.)

The establishment of a central authority also helps even when there is not a police officer on every corner. In a community where it is every man or woman for themselves, there is less trust among its members. But a central authority that dispenses punishments in equal measure may engender a higher level of trust between individuals. If the rules enforced by a legitimate central authority are perceived to be generally unbiased, then people are more likely to adhere to agreed-on standards of behavior.[10]

The critical role a strong central authority plays in preventing wars of attrition from spreading within a community can be seen in the example of failed states. Countries in which a group possesses a coercive force comparable to the amount held by the state are often characterized by excessive violence. Within parts of Syria and Iraq, for example, in which the central authority's capability for coercion is less than other entities', theft, kidnapping, assault, and murder are prevalent. In the past, even some American cities have been engulfed in lawlessness for similar reasons. During Prohibition in the 1920s, Chicago was racked with violence, as bootleggers funded gangs of heavily armed men who deployed coercive force comparable to the police.

Our ancestors figured out long ago that the formation of large communities without a strong central authority leads to internal wars of attrition. They realized that all-pay auctions, in the form of violence between community members, typically result in ruinous outcomes. Hence the rise of states with strong central authorities to administer justice.

The TV Remote and Relationships

In physical battles between individuals, both incur the cost of fighting, such as injuries and potentially death, regardless of the eventual victor. The same applies to the emotional costs incurred in verbal conflicts.

Couples may argue over control of the TV remote to determine which movie to watch. At the end of the discussion, both have suffered the emotional drain of trying to convince the love of their life that a particular film will be highly enjoyable. Just as in any war of attrition, the stress from arguing over the last five minutes is a sunk cost, so the incremental anguish of spending another five minutes squabbling seems justified.

But half an hour later, with no decision made, the toll on the relationship has now far exceeded the additional value to either party from watching the film of their choice. Nevertheless, both sides continue to argue, just like the Allied and Central armies in World War I fought on until men and materials were completely exhausted.

Rather than fight all the time, couples would save themselves a lot of aggravation (and counseling fees) by adopting optimal mixed strategies. Just as with two warring nations, how often to fight depends on the value of the prize, the cost of battle, and the odds of winning.

The cost of spending the next two hours suffering through a movie you do not want to watch is relatively high compared with two more minutes of quarreling. Recall that if the incremental bid cost is less than the value of the item at auction, then it is worth it to keep bidding, or in this case, continue arguing. But this leads to the ruinous outcome in which hours later you are still arguing about what movie to watch.

Let's assume the odds of winning the argument are fifty-fifty and the relative payoffs and costs, measured in terms of the pleasure of watching a movie of your choice and the psychological stress from quarreling, are comparable to those of the warlike and peaceful nations above. As before, the optimal mixed strategy is to fight five out of every six times.

Different assumptions on the value of watching a favored film, the cost of arguing, and the odds of winning will change the calculus concerning the optimal mixed strategy. If one party does not really care that much about which movie to watch, then they should rarely argue (the lower the value of a prize, the less often you should fight). If the emotional drain to one party is much greater than to the other, then that party also should argue less (the higher the cost of battle, the less frequently you should fight). If one party never gives in, then the cost of battle is infinite, and there is no point in arguing at all.

A factor that scrambles the calculation of an optimal mixed strategy in terms of gaining control of the remote is marriage.

When arguing about which movie to watch, a marriage license is kind of like a strong central authority. The overwhelming force of the emotional and financial costs of divorce, not to mention the collateral damage to the kids, discourages couples from moving the argument from the living room to the courtroom over a rom-com versus *John Wick* (a personal favorite of mine).

Of course, every couple has a different calculus.

I have watched all three *John Wick*s. On my own time.

Conclusions

World War I was an example of a war of attrition. Once begun, trench warfare waged for years, even after it became clear that the losses from the battle exceeded the gains from victory. This is because wars of attrition are equivalent to an all-pay auction in which the item to be won is victory and the cost of bidding is measured in men and materials. Game theory predicts that wars of attrition, like all-pay auctions, frequently end in ruinous outcomes. In theory, two players should be able to exist in a state of equilibrium, avoiding ruinous wars of attrition, if both adopt an optimal mixed strategy. In practice, warlike players periodically test others, and peaceful players are forced to sometimes fight back, employing a mixed strategy to prevent repeated extortion.

To avoid wars of attrition between individuals, strong central authorities can, in effect, outbid the violence of any individual or group of individuals within a community. The same principles governing wars of attrition apply to many forms of human conflict, including verbal jousting with those we live with and love. Game theory predicts what we see in the real world: wars of attrition do occur, and when they do, they are frequently ruinous. But players can adopt a mixed strategy and thereby incentivize other players to peacefully coexist. With a knowledge of game theory, we do not have to fight (all the time) over the remote.

Next, we turn from conflicts between nations (and significant others) to elections. One of the first mathematicians to apply game theory to elections was a professor who would later go on to become one of the world's most famous authors. This mathematician applied game theory to elections during the late 1860s partly to spite his boss, the dean of his college. In June 1863, the dean had abruptly cut off all contact between the mathematician and the dean's daughter.

The mathematician's pen name was Lewis Carroll, and the dean's daughter was Alice.

CHAPTER 7

Elections: Spoilers, Cycling, and Ice Cream Stands

Charles Dodgson: Alice and a New Method of Voting

Charles Dodgson (1832–1898) was a mathematician, an ordained deacon of the Church of England, a photographer, and a writer.[1] He was most famous for having authored *Alice's Adventures in Wonderland* and the sequel *Through the Looking-Glass* under the pen name Lewis Carroll.

Dodgson was born in Cheshire, the third of eleven children. His father was the archdeacon of Richmond, a senior post in the Church of England, and his mother died when Dodgson was a teenager. Educated at Oxford, Dodgson graduated first in his class in mathematics and accepted a post as a lecturer at his alma mater, where he studied and taught for the next twenty-six years. He published a dozen books in the fields of geometry, matrix algebra, and logic. The Dodgson condensation is still used today as a method of evaluating determinants. Dodgson invented truth trees, the basis for parts of modern symbolic logic.

In 1856, Dodgson was in his second year of teaching when Henry Liddell arrived to assume the position of dean of Christ Church and vice-chancellor of Oxford University. Liddell was accompanied by his wife, Lorina, and their children, Harry, Lorina, Edith, and four-year-old Alice. Dodgson quickly developed a friendship with the Liddell family and regularly took the children on rowing trips on nearby waterways. On July 4, 1862, Dodgson took the three sisters, including ten-year-old Alice, boating on a stretch of river between Oxford and Godstow. During this outing, the thirty-year-old Dodgson improvised a story about a little girl who fell down a rabbit hole. That story later evolved into the Alice books.

During the last week of June 1863, Dodgson had a falling out with Dean Liddell, after an outing on the nearby waterway with Alice and her sisters, and never again was permitted to take the children on excursions. He sent the first draft of the manuscript of *Alice's Adventures in Wonderland* to Alice as a Christmas present in 1864, but the Liddells never acknowledged the gift.[2] The Liddells also burned all of Dodgson's letters to Alice.[3] Near the end of her life, Mrs. Liddell forbade the family biographer from mentioning Dodgson's name.[4]

With the publication of *Alice's Adventures in Wonderland* in 1865 and *Through the Looking-Glass* in 1871, Dodgson became an internationally known writer. However, the Liddells continued to prevent Dodgson from spending time with their kids, even though Dodgson and the dean worked together.

In retaliation, Dodgson sought to undermine the dean.

Dean Liddell had commissioned a new belfry for Christ Church. Dodgson, now a famous author, responded with a satirical pamphlet, *The New Belfry*, in which he described the proposed design chosen by Liddell as "Early Debased." This prompted the Oxford architectural committee to hold a new contest for the design of the structure. To thwart Dean Liddell's influence, Dodgson designed an innovative voting system that effectively diluted the power of the dean over the members of the committee. Dodgson proposed the adoption of a form of ranked-choice voting—what became known in game theory as the Dodgson method—and in the process he excoriated the "extraordinary injustice" of the plurality voting system previously used by the committee.[5] Given Dodgson's fame as a writer and his reputation as a first-rate mathematician, the committee adopted the Dodgson method, which muted Dean Liddell's control over the redesign of the belfry.

One biographer later wrote that Dodgson "had also in a curious way placed himself above Liddell, temporarily, as it were, usurping the functions of the Dean; for while the Dean presided officially, [Dodgson] had chosen the procedure that the Governing Body would follow."[6]

In subsequent years, Dodgson would further develop the Dodgson method for voting. A common theme of his work on the game theory of elections was to limit the control of a dominant political party (or person) over a decision-making process. Dodgson would vociferously advocate, sometimes successfully, for adoption of the Dodgson method during his remaining years at Oxford in matters such as budget approvals and the hiring of new professors, much to the displeasure of Dean Liddell.

The falling out between Dodgson and Dean Liddell was well known at the time, but the exact reasons remain unclear to this day. It has been alleged that Dodgson acted inappropriately toward Alice or one of her sisters.

While claiming to be prudish, the Victorians were not above exploiting young girls. In 1275, the age of consent in England was set at twelve and did not increase to thirteen until 1875. Dodgson's brother proposed to a girl who was fourteen. Given the limited economic opportunities for women during this time, girls were often forced to marry early, frequently at the urging of their parents. At the time of the split with the Liddells in 1863, Alice was approaching twelve years of age, and Dodgson was just an unknown, poor Oxford math professor—the Alice books would not be published until almost two years later. The Liddells may have simply decided to cut off a budding relationship that they did not favor. But given the mores of the time, it seems strange the Liddells would have reacted so strongly if Dodgson's advances were appropriate. The Liddells could have simply told Dodgson they did not approve of the match.

And Dodgson did seem fascinated with young girls.

Dodgson was an early adopter of the new technology of photography and began taking photographs in the 1860s. Dodgson took more than three thousand photographs during his life, but at least two-thirds of them were destroyed either by Dodgson or by his family after his death. Of the surviving images, over half were of children, some nude or semi-nude.[7] Among these photographs is one of a six-year-old Alice, posed in a tattered dress hanging low off her shoulder.[8] As he grew older, Dodgson seemed to have realized these photographs were inappropriate. In 1881, he wrote to one of the mothers of the girls he had photographed years earlier:

> Would you like to have any more copies of the
> full front photographs of the children? I intend to
> destroy all but one of each. That is all that I want
> for myself, and, though I consider them perfectly
> innocent in themselves, there is really no friend to

*whom I should wish to give photographs which so
entirely defy conventional rules.*[9]

In fact, Dodgson explicitly asked the executors of his will to
destroy any remaining nude prints after his death.[10]

Dodgson was a prolific writer who chronicled his life in thirteen
bound volumes of diaries. However, four volumes disappeared
between his death and when his family turned over the diaries
to the British Museum in 1969.[11] In addition, ten pages from the
extant volumes were cut out by a razor or knife.[12] In particular,
the diary entries around the time of his break with the Liddells
are missing. Page 91 of Journal 8, covering June 27–29, 1863, the
period after his last boating excursion with the Liddell sisters on
June 25, was removed. Dodgson does not mention Alice or her
sisters again until December 30, when Dodgson records that he is
still keeping his distance from the girls.[13]

In 1930, Alice's sister Lorina was questioned about Dodgson in
a private interview. Just before Lorina died, she felt compelled to
write to Alice and reveal what she had said:

*I said his manner became too affectionate to you
as you grew older and that mother spoke to him
about it and that offended him, so he ceased coming to visit us again, as one had to find some reason
for all intercourse ceasing.*[14]

Dodgson never married. Later in life, he retired on the roy-
alties from the Alice books and maintained his office at Oxford,
where his windows overlooked the gardens of the deanery where
Alice Liddell had played as a child. Dodgson died from pneumo-
nia on January 14, 1898, and Dean Liddell passed four days later.
Alice Liddell would live for another thirty-six years. In 1928,

Alice Liddell sold the manuscript that Dodgson had given her at a Sotheby's auction for £15,400 to stave off poverty.[15] She said at the time, "I am tired of being Alice in Wonderland. Does it sound ungrateful? It is. Only I do get tired."[16]

From 1873 to 1876, Dodgson wrote three pamphlets on elections that have been described as "one of the two most distinguished contributions to the Theory of Committees and Elections that have ever been made."[17] Dodgson's derivation of the Dodgson method for voting is couched in mathematics that is beyond the scope of this book. However, his basic idea was to replace plurality voting with a version of what today is called ranked-choice voting.

To understand the differences between plurality and ranked-choice voting, some background about the game theory of elections is required.

Plurality and Ranked-Choice Voting: Spoiler Alert

In plurality voting, the winner is the candidate with the most votes. In elections with two candidates, the results from a plurality vote reflect the views of the majority. In elections with more than two candidates, this is not always the case.

To illustrate, assume there are three candidates: A, B, and C. Candidates A and B are liberals, although A is more liberal than B, and candidate C is a conservative. In an election, A and B receive 40 percent and 15 percent of the vote, respectively, and C receives the remaining 45 percent. Although 55 percent of the electorate is liberal, the conservative candidate wins the election, as they have garnered the most votes. B is considered a "spoiler," siphoning off liberal votes from A, resulting in a victory for C. If given a choice, a majority of voters, who are liberal, would have preferred either A or B over C.

Ranked-choice voting attempts to fix the problem of spoilers by allowing voters to express a preference among the candidates.

Each voter is asked to rank the candidates in order of preference. In our example, most liberal voters will favor A over B and B over C. Conservative voters will favor C over B and B over A.

To count the votes, each candidate faces off against the others in a two-way election. In this example, it is assumed that the liberals will vote for the more liberal candidate and the conservatives will vote for the more conservative candidate. The candidate who defeats all of the other candidates in these two-way elections is declared the winner.

In a two-way election, A will defeat C (55 percent to 45 percent), as the liberal supporters of A and B will vote for A. But A will lose to B (40 percent to 60 percent) because the conservative supporters of C will prefer B over A. C cannot defeat A (45 percent to 55 percent) or B (45 percent to 55 percent) because liberals, who are a majority, prefer A or B over C. However, B will defeat A and C. B is the only one of the three candidates who wins all two-way elections. Therefore, under ranked-choice voting, B will be declared the winner.

Because of the presence of a spoiler, candidate B, in the race, plurality voting resulted in the election of the conservative C, even though a majority of the electorate is liberal. Using ranked-choice voting, B is elected because they are the only candidate favored by the electorate in head-to-head pairings of the candidates.

But Dodgson realized there was a potential problem with ranked-choice voting. Variations in the percentage of votes each candidate receives means that scenarios are possible in which no candidate can defeat all the others. In this case, the pair-wise elections in which candidates face off against each other continue without end and no overall winner can be determined. Dodgson labeled this "cycling."

Dodgson never found a satisfactory solution to the problem of cycling. Under the Dodgson method, if no candidate can defeat all others in a two-way contest, then the best Dodgson could come up with was to say the winner was the candidate who won the greater number of the head-to-head contests.[18] But this means that the winner will have lost at least one of the head-to-head elections. This defeats the original purpose of the Dodgson method, which was to produce a candidate that a majority of voters would all agree on, if forced to choose between just two candidates.

It is worth noting that in one of his pamphlets Dodgson lays out his method in terms that are strikingly similar to a Nash equilibrium, some eight decades before the Princeton PhD candidate published his groundbreaking paper. Dodgson stated that the reason his method was superior to plurality voting was that, if given a chance to change their ballots post-election, voters would have no regrets. This is equivalent to a Nash equilibrium: no player will change their strategy given knowledge of the strategies of others after the game is concluded. In our example, the Dodgson method is superior to a plurality election because, in the plurality election, if given a chance to recast their ballots after the victory of conservative candidate C, liberal voters would change their strategy to avoid splitting their votes between candidates A and B. Unlike Nash, Dodgson did not prove this mathematically, but the basic idea is there.

Dodgson expressed his frustration numerous times in his diaries over his inability to find a ranked-choice voting system that did not cycle. In 1877, he wrote, "A really scientific method for arriving at the result which is, on the whole, most satisfactory to a body of electors, seems to still be a desideratum."[19]

But cycling is not the main problem, in my opinion, with the Dodgson method. In our example, the candidate (B) with the least support among the public (15 percent) is declared the winner. This outcome would be counterintuitive to most voters. An election mechanism in which the spoiler is declared the victor would seem to be fundamentally flawed.

Imagine that the Dodgson method had been used in the 2000 US presidential election. As a percentage of the popular vote, Bush, Gore, and Nader received 47.9, 48.4, and 2.7 percent, respectively. As we discuss later in the chapter, Ralph Nader, the Green Party candidate, most likely played the role of spoiler, putting Florida in the win column for Bush and handing Bush the presidency. Let's assume liberal voters preferred Nader over Bush and conservative voters favored Nader over Gore. Using the Dodgson method in a national direct popular vote among the three candidates (bypassing the Electoral College for this example), Nader would have become the forty-third president of the United States.

To fix the spoiler-as-winner problem, some game theorists contend that approval voting is superior to the Dodgson method.

Approval Voting: Spoilers Are Still Winners

With approval voting, individuals cast either an approve or disapprove vote for each candidate. Voters are free to vote to approve or disapprove some or all of the candidates. The candidate with the highest number of total approval votes is declared the winner. The basic idea is that the more popular candidates are likely to receive more approval votes than the spoilers.

But that may not always be the case.

Suppose those who support A in our example only cast approval votes for other liberals such as B. But those who support C also cast approval votes for the less liberal B. In this case, B would receive approval votes from 100 percent of the population and once again win the election, and the spoiler-as-winner problem has not been fixed.

In fact, it could even be much worse.

Assume that 98 percent of all voters are supporters of liberal A, and the remaining 2 percent are split evenly between less liberal B and conservative C. Liberals cast approval ballots for A and

B, and supporters of C cast their approval votes for C and the less liberal B. Therefore, B receives approval votes from 100 percent of voters, compared with 99 percent and 1 percent for A and C, respectively. B, who is the first choice of 1 percent of the population, wins the election.

Hence, approval voting does not fix the spoiler-as-winner problem. The basic flaw with approval voting is that the electorate cannot express a preference between their first and second choices. The ballots cast for A are really first choice and those cast for B are second choice. Yet, under approval voting, those ballots are given equal weight. If the 2000 presidential election had been held by approval rating through a direct popular vote, Ralph Nader may have been elected president.

To solve the spoiler-as-winner problem with approval voting, some game theorists argue for score voting.

Score Voting: Good Enough for Amazon and the Olympics

With score voting, individuals assign candidates a score, frequently on a scale from one to ten. The candidate with the highest average score is declared the winner. Score voting is employed on Amazon to rank goods and services from movies to pencils, and it is used by Olympic judges to award medals to athletes from gymnasts to ice skaters. In theory, score voting solves the problems of spoilers and spoilers-as-winners: the most popular candidate should receive the highest average score.

However, score voting in practice can easily devolve into plurality voting. The optimal strategy with score voting is to rate your candidate the highest and all other candidates the lowest. In our example, if supporters of A, B, and C each give their favored candidate a score of 10 and the others a score of 1, then the candidates will have average scores of 4.6, 2.35, and 5.05, respectively. This is the same outcome as plurality voting, in which the conservative candidate wins although the majority of the electorate is liberal.

Unfortunately, score voting incentivizes voters to select just one candidate by assigning the highest score to their first choice and the lowest score to all the others. Score voting does solve the spoiler-as-winner problem, as the least popular candidate will receive the lowest score. But the spoiler problem remains.

And that is not the only issue with score voting.

Let's return to our example of candidates A, B, and C. Assume that A and C are well known, but B is more of a fringe candidate, and the supporters of A and C do not know enough about B to express an opinion. The supporters of A and C will give high and low marks to their respective candidates and no score to B. Because B will receive no scores from the supporters of A and C and the highest mark from their own supporters, B will emerge victorious with a perfect score of 10.

The proponents of score voting recognize there needs to be a "quota," or minimum percentage of voters who score a candidate for that candidate to win. For example, if the quota is set at 51 percent, then any candidate who is not scored by more than half the voters is eliminated from consideration. Therefore, only a candidate for which at least a majority of the electorate provides a score can emerge victorious.

But voters will recognize that opposing candidates can be knocked out of the race by not scoring them. Go back to our initial example in which voters supported A, B, and C by 40, 15, and 45 percent, respectively. If the supporters of each candidate do not rank the other candidates, then no candidate will be ranked by the required quota of 51 percent of the population. There will be no winner—the equivalent to the problem of cycling we had with ranked-choice voting and the Dodgson method.

To solve this problem with score voting, the percentage of

voters required to rank a candidate for that candidate to win could be reduced. Let's say the quota is set at 30 percent. In our example, withholding a score will not affect the outcome of the election, as A and C will be ranked by more than 30 percent of the population. But then C will win, and we again have the spoiler problem.

Recognizing the problems with plurality voting, ranked-choice voting, the Dodgson method, approval voting, and score voting, many game theorists have recommended instant runoff voting (IRV).

Instant Runoff Voting: Fewer Spoilers and No Cycling

With IRV, like in the Dodgson method, voters rank candidates in order of preference. If a candidate is the first choice for more than half the voters, then that candidate wins. If not, the candidate with the least number of first-choice votes is eliminated, and that candidate's votes are reallocated to the other candidates according to the second choices on those ballots. Then the process starts again until there are only two candidates remaining.

In our example, B is eliminated with only 15 percent of the first-choice votes compared with 40 percent and 45 percent of the first-choice votes for A and C, respectively. The supporters of B marked A, the other liberal candidate, as their second choice, and so the ballots cast for B are reallocated to A. As a result, A now has 55 percent of the votes (the original 40 percent plus the 15 percent reallocated from B). C receives no new votes since C is the third choice of B voters. With only two candidates remaining, A is the winner with 55 percent of the votes compared with C, who has just 45 percent. In this example, IRV solves the spoiler and spoiler-as-winner problems, resulting in the election of A, the non-spoiler candidate who represents the liberal majority.

In addition, IRV solves the cycling problem. By eliminating

one candidate at a time, the IRV process eventually stops, yielding a definitive winner. By contrast, ranked-choice voting can cycle indefinitely, unable to resolve the conflicting outcomes from a series of simultaneous two-way contests. The Dodgson method stops cycling, but at the cost of declaring a winner that a majority of the population may not favor in all two-way contests.

Nevertheless, IRV is not a perfect voting system. While it is more resistant to spoilers, it is not immune.

In our example, suppose supporters of C realized that under IRV their candidate was guaranteed to lose the election. As conservatives, the supporters of C would prefer the less liberal B. Thus, the supporters of C could cast all of their first-choice votes for B, assuring that B would be elected with 60 percent of the initial votes. In this case, C is the spoiler, resulting in the election of B. Nevertheless, it is uncommon for voters to ditch their preferred candidate just to elect another one. The supporters of C would need to agree to support B, which defeats the primary purpose of the political campaign of C. Imagine the conservative party of C hosting a fundraiser for the liberal candidate B.

IRV is also subject to "ballot exhaustion." Assume that there are ten candidates in an election. Some voters most likely will not have an opinion on all ten candidates, perhaps ranking only the top five. If those five are eliminated in the early rounds, then their vote will be exhausted and will not factor into the election of the eventual winner. Studies have shown that ballot exhaustion in IRV elections often affects around 10 percent of the electorate.[20]

However, for a ballot to be exhausted, the voter probably did not express a preference on one of the leading candidates, who are generally the most well known. In addition, the voter consciously chose not to rank all contenders. I suspect in these instances voters are indeed expressing a preference, which is an indifference to candidates they do not rank.

As we have seen, IRV is not without its issues.[21] Voters can manipulate IRV, selecting as first choice their second-choice candidate, just like in the case of plurality and other voting systems. The ballots of some voters can be exhausted and thus not count in the election returns.

Dodgson was neither the first nor the last mathematician to employ game theory to try to formulate an election mechanism that consistently yielded an outcome that reflected the will of the average voter. In the thirteenth century, the mathematician and Catholic priest Ramon Llull advocated that the Roman Catholic Church adopt something comparable to ranked-choice voting in the election of the pope and other high church officials. During the eighteenth century, two French philosophers and mathematicians, the Marquis de Condorcet and Jean-Charles de Borda, did the same for their country.

But there is a reason Dodgson and others were never able to devise the perfect voting system.

Arrow's Impossibility Theorem

During the 1940s, an American economist, Kenneth Arrow, took a different approach to elections and won a Nobel Prize in 1972 for his efforts. Rather than try to find an optimal election mechanism, Arrow set out to show that no such system was possible. In 1948, he published a paper that proved just that, which is known as Arrow's impossibility theorem (AIT).

Arrow was a research associate at the University of Chicago after World War II when he was offered a job at RAND Corporation.[22] He immediately accepted. As he recounted years later:

> *This Air Force thing at that point was a wild, far-out place, open to all kinds of ideas. The idea was that because of the new nature of warfare, particularly*

the bomb, all the old views were wrong. . . . It was
an invitation to take a very wild point of view.[23]

Besides, this was the chance to work with John von Neumann. When von Neumann spoke at RAND, according to Arrow, "everyone sat up in great awe."[24] And he also got to hang out with John Nash and Herman Kahn.

At RAND, Arrow worked on issues related to mutual assured destruction (see Chapter 5). One day he was talking with Olaf Helmer, a political scientist and philosopher in residence at RAND, about how a leader, such as President Truman, could represent the views of the nation on the critical issue of nuclear war. At the time, some believed the United States should launch a preemptive nuclear strike against the Soviet Union and China given that America's military superiority would not last. Others supported containing the spread of communism through the buildup of conventional forces in Europe and Asia. Still others were pacifists arguing for unilateral disarmament. Given the diversity of views within the country, Arrow wondered how a leader could determine the preferences of a majority of the population.

Arrow concluded that there was no optimal system to measure the preferences of an electorate when confronted with more than two policy options or candidates. In 1948, he published the RAND research report, "The Possibility of a Universal Social Welfare Function," in which he stated that "there is no method of aggregating individual preferences which led to a consistent social preference scale."[25] Arrow followed up this paper with his 1951 book, *Social Choice and Individual Values.* While his RAND research paper was not widely read, Arrow's book had a profound effect on many social scientists.

The first utilitarian philosophers, such as Jeremy Bentham and John Stuart Mill, had become convinced in the early nineteenth

century that the goal of government was to bring about the greatest good for the greatest number of people. Many in the West
believed that the will of the majority, reflected through democratic
elections, expressed what was best for the most. But AIT now
proved that there was no reliable way for voters to express their
preferences when given more than two choices between policies
or candidates.

AIT's impact on the social sciences was comparable to the effect
that Kurt Gödel's incompleteness theorems had on philosophy. For
thousands of years, philosophers had been seeking the "truth." In
1931, Gödel's two incompleteness theorems demonstrated that a
complete and consistent set of axioms was impossible. There is no
such thing as the truth if a set of beliefs cannot be proven to be
without internal contradiction. Similarly, in 1948, Arrow demonstrated there is no set of preferences among individuals confronted
with more than two choices that is necessarily internally consistent. But the goal of social science is to achieve the greatest good
for the greatest number. AIT showed that this objective may be
forever unobtainable since preferences of a group of individuals
cannot be shown to be free from contradiction.

The math behind AIT is complicated. What is important for
our purposes is that AIT demonstrates that the preferences of voters when choosing among more than two candidates will at times
suffer from inconsistencies, such as spoilers or spoilers-as-winners.
In effect, Arrow proved that all voting systems have flaws.

Arrow was not claiming that all voting systems will yield outcomes all the time that do not represent the will of the average voter.
Similarly, Gödel did not claim that all systems of beliefs are incon-
sistent. But just as Gödel showed that there are no sets of statements
that can be proved to be free from internal contradictions, Arrow
demonstrated that there are no voting systems that are free from
problems, such as spoilers, spoilers-as-winners, and cycling.

As Arrow said about AIT: "Most systems are not going to work badly all the time. All I proved is that all can work badly at times."[26]

Many game theorists such as Dodgson sought to construct the perfect voting system and eventually gave up. AIT proved that Dodgson and others had set for themselves an impossible task.

Voting Methods: Five Enter, Two Leave

In my view, when designing election systems, we should not let the perfect become the enemy of the good. AIT teaches us that every voting mechanism has flaws. However, we can set out some basic minimum requirements for an acceptable voting system.

First, a voting system should yield a winner. After all, that is the purpose of an election. As we have seen, ranked-choice voting is subject to cycling, in which no winner can be determined. The Dodgson method attempts to remedy this flaw by picking the candidate that wins the most head-to-head elections. But even Dodgson was unhappy with this partial solution. The goal of ranked choice is to select a candidate that a majority of voters favor, given a choice of any two candidates. Ranked-choice voting and the Dodgson method fail to meet that objective. Because these two systems do not always produce a clear winner, they do not meet the basic minimum criteria for an acceptable voting mechanism.

Second, a voting system should not allow a candidate with a majority of first-choice votes to lose an election. Under approval voting, we showed an example of a candidate with 99 percent of the first-choice votes losing to a candidate with 1 percent of the first-choice votes. Under score voting, we also saw how a candidate who is effectively the first choice of 1 percent of the electorate would be declared the winner in the absence of a quota. If quotas are imposed, then score voting may not yield a winner, and we are back to the same problem of cycling that plagues ranked-choice voting and the Dodgson method. Hence, approval and score voting are also unacceptable voting mechanisms.

So we are left with plurality voting and IRV.

The main disadvantage of plurality voting is the problem of spoilers. If spoilers are rare in practice, then the advantages of IRV are largely theoretical.

But spoilers are not uncommon. Consider US presidential elections.

Spoilers: More Than One in Five US Presidential Elections

Most people view US politics as a two-party system. In fact, national third-party candidates are not uncommon in US presidential elections.

The 2000 presidential election is one example.

In this election, held on November 7, 2000, George Bush received 2,912,790 votes and Al Gore received 2,912,253 votes in Florida.[27] A difference of 537 votes cost Al Gore the presidency, tipping the Sunshine State into the win column for George Bush. The Green Party candidate, Ralph Nader, received 97,488 votes.[28]

Many independent analyses concluded that Gore would have carried Florida if Nader had not run.[29] A poll in 2000 revealed that if Nader had not run, 45 percent of his voters would have voted for Gore, 27 percent would have voted for Bush, and the rest would not have voted.[30] If the Nader votes were reallocated to Bush and Gore in those proportions, Al Gore would have been the forty-third president of the United States. (Nader has always denied that he cost Democrats the presidency, and counterfactual histories by nature admittedly have a degree of uncertainty. But I believe Gore would have won if Nader had dropped out of the race and endorsed him.)

Other US presidential elections have had even stronger third-party candidates. Nader garnered only 2.7 percent of the popular vote nationwide in 2000. But twelve times in US history a third-party candidate has earned more than 5 percent of the total popular or electoral votes—or 21 percent of all US presidential elections. This does not mean that in all twelve instances the third-party candidate played the role of spoiler. Credible polling data about those who voted for third-party candidates is unavailable for all but the most recent elections. But third-party candidates have siphoned off significant numbers of votes from the two major parties in one in five US presidential contests.

The role of spoilers is even more pronounced in primaries in which there are frequently more than two candidates. One example is the primary for the 2016 US Republican presidential nominee.

The 2016 Republican Primary: Most against One

In March 2015, before Donald Trump announced his candidacy, a poll was taken to assess support for the leading contenders for the 2016 Republican presidential nomination—Jeb Bush, Scott Walker, Ted Cruz, and Chris Christie.[31] The question asked was "If the only two candidates for the Republican nomination were _____ and _____, who would you choose?"

In this head-to-head comparison between the four candidates, no candidate won them all. Therefore, based on those results, an election at that time using ranked choice would have cycled, and there would have been no winner. (The published results of this poll do not reveal enough information to determine who would have been declared the winner under the Dodgson method.) The only candidate who did not cycle was Chris Christie, who lost to all of the other candidates in head-to-head contests.

Future president Trump announced his candidacy three months later on June 16, after descending the escalator at Trump Tower.

His candidacy scrambled the Republican primary. By March 2016, the leading contenders for the Republican presidential nomination were Donald Trump, Ted Cruz, and Marco Rubio. In a poll conducted with the same methodology as the one above, no candidate won all pairings. Once again, a ranked-choice vote would not have determined a winner.[32] But one candidate did not cycle: Trump would have lost to Cruz and Rubio in head-to-head contests. This poll showed, however, that Trump was the victor in a plurality vote with 34 percent compared to Cruz and Rubio at 25 percent and 18 percent, respectively, with other candidates filling out the balance of the field.

The March 2016 poll demonstrated that, while Trump was the first choice of one-third of Republican primary voters, he was not the first or second choice of the remaining two-thirds. If those preferences were maintained throughout the rest of the primary season, then Trump would not have been the nominee under ranked choice, the Dodgson method, or IRV.

The 2016 Republican primaries showed that most primary voters would have preferred a candidate other than the one chosen as the nominee. But plurality voting allows voters to express only their first choice. IRV solves this problem by allowing voters to express not only their first choice but also their second, third, and fourth choices, and so on, among candidates.

I will argue later in the chapter that plurality voting is part of the reason for the poisoned politics in the United States. I will also try to persuade you that adopting IRV will help heal today's partisan political divide.

But first we should address the issue of primaries.

Many believe that a primary system pushes both Democratic and Republican candidates to extremes to win over their respective caucuses. Once committed to extreme positions, candidates struggle to pivot back to more moderate positions in the general election without risking a falloff in turnout among their more partisan supporters. Those who oppose the primary system frequently also support IRV. Many argue there should be no primaries and only one general election with all parties participating. They believe this would result not only in less negative campaigning but also in the election of more moderate candidates.

I wish this were true, but it is not quite that simple.

The economist who first pointed out the complexity and unpredictability of elections with more than two candidates was a professor who taught and inspired Kenneth Arrow to apply his knowledge of mathematics to real-world problems, such as voter preferences.

This professor had an economic law named after him that related to ice cream stands.

Hotelling's Law: More Than Two Is Too Many

Harold Hotelling was a statistician and economist who is most famous for Hotelling's law, a principle he wrote about in the 1920s and 1930s. The basic idea is that if two companies dominate a market, then they will make their products as similar as possible. If there are more than two companies, then product differentiation is the best strategy. Hotelling's law explained the similarity of products in duopolies and the marked differences in goods in more competitive markets.

Near the end of his seminal 1929 article, "Stability in Competition," Hotelling added three sentences about elections.

He wrote that his law was "strikingly exemplified" in politics:

> The competition for votes between Republican and Democratic parties does not lead to a clear drawing of issues. . . . Instead, each party strives to make its platform as much like the others as possible. . . .

*Each candidate "pussyfoots," replies ambiguously
to questions, refuses to take a definite stand in any
controversy for fear of losing votes.*[33]

An example of Hotelling's law in action is two ice cream stands
(A and B) on a boardwalk lining a beach. Assume A is to the left
of center of the beach and B to the right. The two stands offer the
same brand of ice cream, so beachgoers will only patronize the closest stand. Further assume that there are just enough beachgoers to
support two ice cream stands.

The owner of A realizes that they will get all the beachgoers
to their left and those halfway between their stand and stand B.
By moving A to the right toward B, the owner of A can attract
even more customers without losing any customers on the left.
So the owner of A moves their stand toward B. The owner of B
will reason similarly and move their stand to the left toward A.
Eventually, A and B will be right next to each other, straddling a
line that marks the midpoint of the beach. (This also explains why
one intersection sometimes has more than one Starbucks.)

The same logic applies to political candidates. By moving to the
center, a candidate can attract more voters without losing those
farther away on their side of the political spectrum. Hence, in a
two-party system, the tendency is for both parties to veer toward
the middle.[34]

Let's add a third ice cream stand to the boardwalk and assume
there are enough beachgoers to sustain three ice cream stands. We
now have ice cream stands A, B, and C, situated from left to right
facing the beach. Per Hotelling's law, the owner of A will still have
an incentive to move to the right toward B and the owner of C will
move to the left toward B. Eventually, all three ice cream stands
will be right next to each other at the center of the beach.

But B will soon be out of business, supported only by those lined up directly in front of their ice cream stand. So B decides to move to the left of A, and soon A is in financial trouble. To stay in business, A must move either to the left of B or to the right of C. According to Hotelling's law, once there are three or more stands, there is no longer a stable equilibrium, and the shuffling back and forth along the boardwalk will continue indefinitely.

As you may have already guessed, the analogy of ice cream stands on the left, right, and center of a boardwalk applies equally to political candidates and parties. Movements by liberal and conservative candidates toward the center of the political spectrum in races with more than two candidates can squeeze out moderates. But as candidates move toward the center, that opens room for those on the extreme left and right. If a new candidate emerges on the far right, then a candidate to the right of center may move further to the right, as there are more voters to be gained to their right than to their left.

This jockeying for position characterizes elections with more than two candidates. Fundamentally, elections with more than two candidates (or parties) are both more unstable and more likely to give rise to extremists on the left and right of the political spectrum. As one prominent game theorist on elections has written: "If more than two parties or candidates are expected, then the voting-maximizing position is not close to your opponents, but well away from them."[35]

Applied to politics, Hotelling's law predicts that the more candidates in a contest, the less moderate some candidates will be and the more unpredictable the outcome of an election. In the analogy of ice creams stands on a boardwalk lining a beach, the more stands, the more spread out they will be. And nobody knows where a particular stand will end up when the sun goes down.

The power of Hotelling's law has been demonstrated in

computer simulations of plurality elections. In one simulation, ten thousand hypothetical voters participated in two primaries, each with ten candidates, using plurality voting.[36] The electorate was divided into three partisan affiliations: left, right, and independent. A voter was assumed to support the candidate that was the closest to their political views. The candidates' positions along the political spectrum were drawn from a normal distribution centered on the median voter of each party. Not surprisingly, the authors of the study determined that "if there are three or more candidates, there is no single determinate equilibrium."[37]

More disturbing was that candidates on the political extremes often won these hypothetical primary elections. After running hundreds of simulations, the researchers found that candidates frequently did not adopt positions near those of the median voter for their party. Rather, the researchers observed that "electoral competition [of more than two candidates] acts to ensure that extremist candidates will appear."[38] The authors concluded that the key result of the study was

> *the complete unpredictability of the outcomes of a sequence of primaries: the winner of the primary, or the party's nominee, varied as much as two standard deviations from the median partisan voter. The reason is that the median, or any other measure of the center of the distribution of voters, is of little value in predicting the outcome.*[39]

According to the authors of the study, the results of the simulation were comparable to those of "poorly designed lotteries, due to the unstable and unpredictable nature of a primary with multiple candidates."[40]

Hotelling's law shows that in an election between one liberal and one conservative candidate, both will tend to move toward the political center and remain there, just like two ice cream stands on a beach. The moderating influence of Hotelling's law does not apply to elections with more than two candidates, as more extreme candidates will emerge, jockeying for the maximum amount of space along the political spectrum.

Primaries: Part of the Solution

Primary elections are the equivalent of placing a high fence down the center of a beach and thus cutting in half the number of competing ice cream stands. Bathers on each side of the fence can walk only to the ice cream stand on their half of the boardwalk. Assuming there is only enough demand for ice cream to support two stands, competition will winnow down the number of stands to one on the left and one on the right side of the fence. Once the fence comes down, the two remaining stands will move back to the center of the boardwalk.

The same logic applies to elections. In primaries under a two-party system, Democratic and Republican candidates fight it out in their respective primaries, and a winner from each eventually emerges. Once the primaries are over, the winning Democratic and Republican candidates move back toward the political center. As demonstrated above, voter preferences can be readily expressed without inconsistencies in an election between two candidates. With just two candidates, plurality voting works just as well as any voting system. But with more than two candidates, the problems of spoilers, spoilers-as-winners, and cycling arise, and AIT comes into play.

Hence, primaries can be thought of as an attempt to fix the main problem with plurality voting. Eliminating primaries would only add more candidates to the general election, resulting in greater instability and a greater number of extreme candidates.

The Electoral College: Unfair and Unchangeable

Those who support eliminating primaries frequently argue that while reforming US elections, we should also get rid of the Electoral College.

Today, the candidate who receives a majority of the Electoral College vote becomes the US president. There are 538 electors, equal to the total number of senators and representatives from each state, plus three from the District of Columbia. With the exception of Maine and Nebraska, states award Electoral College votes on a winner-take-all basis after a plurality vote. Consequently, third-party candidates rarely receive Electoral College votes. The last third-party US presidential candidate to receive any Electoral College votes was George Wallace in 1968, winning the five southern states of Alabama, Arkansas, Georgia, Louisiana, and Mississippi. This winner-take-all system at the state level means that most voters realize that a third-party vote is wasted. Hence, the US presidential race for practical purposes is generally between the two major party candidates.

Those who support eliminating the Electoral College contend that the current system allows the election of a candidate who finishes second in the popular vote. In fact, this has occurred five times in US history: 1824, 1876, 1888, 2000, and 2016.

This is partly due to the apportionment of electors: each state has two senators and at a minimum one congressperson, regardless of population. Thus, small states have a disproportionate share of the Electoral College. For example, California has a population of 39.3 million and fifty-five electoral votes, while Wyoming has 0.5 million individuals and three electoral votes. In terms of the US presidential election, the vote of an individual in Wyoming is equal to that of 4.3 Californians.

Another factor is the impact of awarding electors within forty-eight of the fifty states on a winner-take-all basis. A party whose voters reside in states that are more politically imbalanced is at a disadvantage. Consider the 2020 US presidential election and the vote totals in Massachusetts and Ohio. In overwhelmingly Democratic Massachusetts, Biden received 2.3 million votes compared with Trump's 1.1 million and gained the state's eleven Electoral College votes. In Ohio, which is more evenly divided politically, Biden and Trump garnered 2.6 million and 3.1 million votes respectively, earning Trump the state's eighteen Electoral College votes. Between the two states, Biden won 54 percent of the popular vote and 38 percent of the Electoral College vote.[41]

But we cannot conclude that the five elections in which the popular and Electoral College votes were in conflict would have yielded different outcomes under a direct popular vote. US presidential campaigns are run with the objective of winning the Electoral College. One analysis wrote that in US presidential campaigns, "four out of five [voters] are absolutely ignored by both campaigns."[42] In 2016, two-thirds of general election campaign spending took place in six states.[43] It does not make sense for a Republican presidential candidate to waste time or money in liberal California or New York.

The counterfactual historical argument that the "wrong" person was elected five times fails to consider that very different campaigns would have been waged by both parties if the goal were to win the popular vote. We cannot know if the first-place finishers, as measured by the popular vote in the 1824, 1876, 1888, 2000, and 2016 presidential elections, would have once again come out on top if the rules of the game had been different.

Proponents of abolishing the Electoral College and implementing a direct popular vote respond that the above is further justification for their position. Today, US presidential elections come down to a handful of swing states: votes in Arizona, Florida, Georgia, Pennsylvania, and Wisconsin matter more than the more populous states of California, Massachusetts, and New York. And the swing states have several counties that largely determine which candidate earns that state's Electoral College votes. Under the current system, a small slice of the American electorate effectively decides who will be the next president.

I can see both sides of the argument. The Electoral College does discourage third-party candidates and thereby tends to force voters into a choice between the two major parties. For all the reasons discussed above, two candidates are better than three or more. On the other hand, the Electoral College may have handed the presidency to the second-place finisher in the past and may do so again in the future. The Electoral College also disenfranchises most voters, sometimes placing the decision on who gets to be the most powerful person on Earth into the hands of those residing in the suburbs of Philadelphia.

But I do not believe this discussion merits a lot of ink. That is because it is highly unlikely the Electoral College will be replaced with a direct popular vote.

Abolishing the Electoral College would require amending the US Constitution. To do so, two-thirds of the states would have to call for a constitutional convention. Once in session, the constitutional convention would have to pass and recommend to the states the adoption of the amendment. Alternatively, the House and Senate, by two-thirds vote of the members of each legislative body, would have to propose such an amendment. Three-fourths of the states (thirty-eight) would then have to ratify the amendment proposed by the constitutional convention or Congress for it to become law.

But a substantial number of states would have no interest in abolishing the Electoral College. Small states would lose the current disproportionate influence they currently enjoy. Swing states would forgo the attention (and promises of political pork) lavished on them every four years. Large Republican-controlled states have never supported eliminating the Electoral College.

Another effort to effectively replace the Electoral College with a direct popular vote is the National Popular Vote Interstate Compact (NPVI). This compact is an agreement among fifteen states and the District of Columbia to cast all their Electoral College votes for the winner of the popular vote if a majority of electors (270) agree to follow their lead. Once again, many small states have no interest in joining the compact. Swing states similarly have no interest in signing up to the NPVI. And Democrats and Republicans are divided on the issue: all fifteen states that have joined the NPVI are solidly Democratic. The NPVI would also be subject to court challenges: legal analysts question whether a state could cast all of its Electoral College votes for a candidate who did not win that state's presidential election.

For these reasons, the Electoral College will be with us for the foreseeable future.

Instant Runoff Voting: The Least Bad Solution

In my opinion, future presidents should be selected by the Electoral College after primaries and a general election that are conducted using IRV.

This proposal has several practical aspects compared with a national popular direct vote. First, the Electoral College is not going away anytime soon. Any reform of US presidential elections that presumes the elimination of the Electoral College is based on an unrealistic assumption. Second, the two major political parties in the US will fight the elimination of primaries.

Fortunately, primaries have a net moderating influence on elections. Ideally, in a two-party system, only two candidates would be on the ballot in November in a US presidential election. As a practical matter, there have always been more than two candidates in the primaries, and there likely always will be. Nevertheless, primaries serve to winnow down the field of presidential hopefuls. Lastly, the states have the sole discretion to choose their respective voting methods. It does not require a constitutional amendment or any federal law for every state to implement IRV.

Furthermore, IRV has another significant benefit: it will help heal the poisoned politics that are sickening our nation. The need for a voting system in the US that encourages moderate, broadly supported candidates is more important than ever. The electorate has become increasingly polarized, resulting in intense political conflict and internal strife.

A fundamental problem with today's plurality voting is it motivates candidates to whip up their supporters against opposing candidates to drive up turnout. Because plurality voting does not allow voters to express anything other than their first choice, candidates focus solely on maximizing the number of first-choice votes. Disparaging the opposing candidates has no consequences, and there is no reason for a candidate to seek a second-choice vote of the supporters of other candidates. By contrast, under IRV, second-choice votes or even third-choice votes can determine an election. As a result, candidates are motivated to campaign less on the negatives about their opponents and more on the positives about themselves. Attacking other candidates has consequences: you may lose the second- or third-choice ballots of your opponent's supporters.

Conclusions

Arrow's impossibility theorem proves that no voting system is perfect. Although it is the best of the lot, IRV still has problems. But its problems are fewer than the other systems and are less of an issue in a two-party system, in which primaries frequently narrow the field before a general election. Even proponents of other nontraditional voting systems would agree that IRV is better than plurality voting.

Our current system of plurality voting incentivizes candidates and parties to get their base out to vote, often at the expense of offending the supporters of their opponents. Under IRV, there is an incentive to gain the second-choice vote of your opponent's supporters. Furthermore, Hotelling's law demonstrates that with just two candidates there is an incentive to move toward the middle, but elections with more than two candidates can lead to victories by those with narrower voter bases. In most cases, IRV stops this from occurring.

We have analyzed IRV and other voting mechanisms in the context of the US presidential elections. However, the same logic applies to other elections that regularly occur throughout the world. From electing legislators to school boards, plurality voting dominates. In addition, these bodies almost universally employ plurality voting to decide policy, which is rarely a choice between only two proposals. The same characteristics that make IRV superior to plurality voting for candidates apply to making decisions on policy matters. IRV works better whenever there is a choice between more than two candidates or policies. We should switch to IRV when selecting our politicians and passing laws at the local and national levels.

An election can be viewed as a type of auction in which voters "bid" for candidates. But the most frequently used auction mechanism in the online world today is nothing like that of any voting system.

The world's most commonly used online auction system was named after an economist who won a Nobel Prize for his work on the applications of game theory to auctions. But he was also known for setting transit fares in New York City and income tax rates in Japan.

CHAPTER 8

Auctions: Shading and Losing by Winning

William Vickrey: Second Price and Subway Fares

William Vickrey (1914–1996) was a Canadian-American economist who was awarded a Nobel Prize for his application of game theory to auctions. Over his lifetime, he published eight books and some 140 articles.[1] A particular type of auction, a sealed-bid second-price auction, is named in his honor, because of his lifelong advocacy of its advantages. Today, the Vickrey auction is the most widely used auction in the online world.

Vickrey was born in British Columbia, but his family moved to New York when he was three months old. He attended Yale, earning a BS in 1935, followed by an MA in economics from Columbia University in 1937. Vickrey was a Quaker and, as a conscientious objector during World War II, spent those years in public service, working for the National Resources Planning Board in Washington, DC, and the Division of Tax Research in the US Department of the Treasury.[2] After the war, he returned to Columbia and earned a PhD in economics in 1948. His 496-page dissertation, "Agenda for Progressive Taxation," is considered one of the blueprints for the policies of progressive taxation that were implemented in the United States during the 1950s and 1960s.[3] He remained at Columbia his entire life and retired from teaching in 1982.

Vickrey was regularly called on by the US government to travel overseas and to advise on taxation. In 1949, he was one of several economists appointed by General Douglas MacArthur, as part of the Shoup Mission, to develop a new tax system for postwar Japan. Vickrey and the other economists believed that a comprehensive reform of the Japanese tax system would promote liberal democracy and a stable economy. These reforms included new measures such as taxing capital gains, adding personal exemptions and deductions, and a wealth tax on fortunes that exceeded five million yen.[4] The Shoup Mission also loosened the iron grip of the central government on tax revenues by granting municipalities greater authority to assess levies on property and enterprises.[5] In subsequent years, Vickrey would undertake similar missions for the US government to Argentina, India, Iran, Liberia, Libya, Venezuela, and Zambia.[6]

Vickrey was also considered the "father of congestion pricing."[7] In 1951, he was tasked by New York City officials with developing a new system of transit fares for subways and buses. He proposed eliminating the existing 15¢ flat fare with fees ranging from 5¢ to 25¢, depending on the time of day.[8] (His recommendations were ignored.) He was also asked to set the pricing for toll roads in the Washington, DC, area. His subsequent report has been described as "almost certainly the most important in urban transport economics over the last quarter century."[9] Vickrey foresaw the equivalent of today's E-ZPass, an electronic device for collecting tolls on freeways. In 1952, he wrote: "One possible detection and billing method would use electronic identifier units carried in each vehicle, which would activate recording devices in or on the road. Computers would sort the information and determine charges; motorists would be billed monthly."[10]

A staunch liberal, Vickrey was an early and vocal advocate for progressive taxation. In 1939, as a research assistant at Columbia, he pioneered the idea of cumulative taxation as an alternative to an annual income tax. Cumulative taxation eliminates the incentives to shift income between calendar years to reduce taxes, a technique employed regularly by the wealthy.[11] Vickrey continued his advocacy for progressive taxation throughout his life. His last paper, "Fifteen Fatal Fallacies of Financial Fundamentalism," a searing criticism of supply-side economics, was published in 1996 six days before his death from a heart attack.[12]

Four Basic Types of Auctions

Auctions are games in which the primary goal is to discover a price at which buyers and sellers will complete a transaction. Auctions would be unnecessary if sellers had complete information. If the prices at which all buyers were willing to transact were known, then a seller could simply approach the buyer willing to pay the highest price. However, in most instances, buyers are unwilling to reveal to the seller the highest price they are willing to pay. Likewise, sellers may be reluctant to reveal the lowest price at which they are willing to sell. So a game is played between buyers and sellers, in the form of an auction, and the outcome of that game determines whether an exchange occurs and at what price. In most cases, buyers surrender money to sellers in return for goods or services, but auctions could also be in the form of barter.

The outcome of an auction for a single item is based on either a first or second price.[13] In a first-price auction, the seller receives the price submitted by the highest bidder. In a second-price auction, the seller gets the price put forward by the second-highest bidder. Buyers can submit either open or sealed bids. Open bids are common in art auctions, where buyers signal their willingness to pay by raising a hand or paddle. Sealed bids are frequently used for government contracts, in which firms submit proposals without publicly disclosing their bids. As a result, auctions can be divided into one of four types: open or sealed first price and open or sealed second price.

Revenue Equivalence: Different Auctions, Same Outcome

In an idealized world, the outcome of all four types of auctions would be the same. Given certain assumptions, all should yield the same price, or what game theorists call "revenue equivalence."

To illustrate, suppose there is one seller (S1) and two buyers (B1 and B2). B1 and B2 are willing to pay $10 and $8, respectively, for the item S1 is selling. B1 and B2 also know what the other bidder is willing to pay, but S1 does not. The smallest bid increment is $0.01. Let's consider in turn each of the four types of auctions.

An open-bid first-price auction is known as a "Dutch" auction, named after how cut flowers have been sold for centuries in the Netherlands. The Bloemenveiling Aalsmeer outside Amsterdam sells more than twenty million flowers and plants daily through an open first-price auction that processes about fifteen hundred transactions per hour.[14] It is a descending-price auction, in which the price starts high and then decreases incrementally on a set schedule until a buyer emerges. An advantage of this type of auction is that it can occur on a set timetable, which is important when selling highly perishable commodities, such as thousands of bundles of cut flowers. In our example, B1 (who is willing to pay up to $10 and knows B2 will only pay up to $8) will wait until the price declines to $8.01 and then bid, winning the auction.

A sealed-bid first-price auction is known as a "pay-what-you-bid" auction. The buyers do not reveal their bids to each other but instead submit the equivalent of sealed envelopes that are opened at the same time. The clearing price is the highest bid. B1 will bid $8.01 (once again knowing that B2 will only pay $8) and win the prize.

An open-bid second-price auction is called an English auction, commonly used by auction houses such as Sotheby's and Christie's. This type is an ascending-price auction, in which the price begins low and then increases until the bids cease. In our example, B2 will drop out after B1 bids $8.01, and B1 will once again win the auction.

A sealed-bid second-price auction is called a Vickrey auction, commonly used by online companies such as Google and eBay. If B1 submits a sealed bid for $10, then B1 will win the auction and pay the $8 bid placed by B2, plus the minimum bid increment for a total of $8.01.

In all four cases, the seller receives $8.01 for the item. However, auctions in the real world are rarely this simple. We will consider several common complicating factors.

Reserve Prices: More Competition

One feature typical of many real-world auctions is a reserve price, a level below which the seller will not transact. In effect, a reserve price is like adding one more bidder to the auction. This has several benefits for the seller and none for the buyers.

The introduction of an additional bidder into the auction means more competition among the buyers. Even if the buyers do not know the reserve price, they know there is now one more bidder out there. That bidder is the seller, who presumably knows more about the item to be auctioned than anybody else.

A reserve price also helps prevent collusion among the buyers. Suppose in our example that B1 and B2 agreed that only one of the two would participate in the auction, bidding a price of $1, and to divide up the item between themselves afterward. To prevent this, the seller could set a reserve price near $8. In addition, the seller can be assumed to be the most well-informed participant in the auction, and by setting a minimum public price, the seller is signaling the value of the item to buyers. However, in some cases, reserve prices are confidential with an option to reduce if necessary, providing the seller with the flexibility to transact depending on how the bidding progresses.

Sellers Prefer Risk-Averse Buyers

Auctions also have participants with varying levels of risk tolerance. Some are risk averse, while others are risk seeking.

Bidders who are risk averse wish to decrease the variability of the outcome. Such bidders will pay more than risk-neutral bidders to increase the odds of winning the auction. But a higher price means a lower expected net gain from the successful acquisition of the item. Similarly, bidders who are risk seeking are willing to accept a greater degree of variability. These bidders will bid less than risk-neutral bidders, decreasing the chances of winning the auction but increasing the net gain in the event they are successful. In effect, submitting a higher price is like buying insurance to protect against losing: the bidder has more certainty about the outcome of the auction, but that comes at the increased cost of the premium paid to increase the odds of winning. Thus, from the perspective of sellers, the greater the number of risk-averse buyers the better. From the perspective of buyers, the opposite is true.

Moral Hazard: Heads I Win, Tails You Lose

Some auctions in the real world come with a moral hazard for the seller. If the seller does not demand payment up front, then the buyers have an incentive to bid more. If the bid is too high, then the buyer can default on the remaining payment, which creates an incentive to submit a higher price.

This is exactly what happened when the US government auctioned off large swaths of the telecommunications spectrum in 1994. To promote mobile telephony and other services, the Federal Communications Commission ran auctions in which many successful bidders were allowed to make a down payment of 10 percent and then pay the balance seven years later. Many of these successful bidders later determined that the value of the spectrum awarded was less than 90 percent of the bid price and declared bankruptcy.[15] As one economist wrote, "The FCC's ham-fisted pursuit of a noble goal destroyed this segment of the auction entirely."[16]

Incomplete Information: To Shade or Not to Shade

Unlike our idealized example, one characteristic of most auctions in the real world is that bidders do not reveal to other bidders the highest price they are willing to pay. In other words, there is incomplete information.

If B1 and B2 have incomplete information, then they have an incentive to reduce or "shade" their respective bids. A bidder will not want to pay the full value of an item if others value it less. For example, the item may be worth $10 to B1, but there is no reason to bid $10 if B1 suspects B2 is willing to pay no more than $8. Hence, B1 has an incentive to bid less than $10. In the case of incomplete information, the price received by the seller is expected to be lower than the value to the highest bidder, even in a first-price auction, as bidders will shade their bids.

A way to discourage bidders from shading their bids is a sealed second-price auction, or Vickrey auction.

Let's consider two cases under a Vickrey auction: B1 wins or B1 loses. If B1 wins, then B1 will pay B2's bid price plus an increment. If B1 loses, then B1 will get no benefit from the auction. If B1 loses because of bidding below $10, then B1 has given up the potential benefit from winning the auction at a price equal to or less than what they were willing to pay. Hence, B1 can always improve their expected outcome by bidding $10. B2 should reason similarly and bid $8.

This is why in Vickrey auctions the optimal strategy is to bid the highest amount you are willing to pay, regardless of what the other bidders do. In a Vickrey auction, there is no advantage to be gained from shading. By contrast, other types of auctions incentivize bidding less than the price you are willing to pay. And this is why Vickrey auctions are particularly favored by many game theorists and economists.

Of the four types of auctions, Vickrey auctions are the most frequently used in the online world. Google uses them to sell advertising through millions of auctions every minute of every day.[17] eBay also employs a version of a Vickrey auction to sell goods, but unlike Google Ads auctions, eBay auctions usually take place over an extended period, anywhere from one to ten days, with the default option of one week.[18]

By using Vickrey auctions, Google and eBay provide potential buyers with a simple and efficient mechanism for submitting bids. There is no need to spend time and money figuring out how to shade bids.

Google Ads Auctions: Fast and Furious

When you query a keyword, Google search engines return a column of site links with a headline and a sentence or two describing the content behind each. Google presents these site links based on organic and paid search results. Organic search results are determined by Google algorithms that rank sites based on the number of links to other sites, relevance as measured by number of similar words in the text, how often visitors click the page, and a host of other criteria. Paid search results are determined based on what advertisers bid and Google's Ad Rank (more on this below).

The order of site links on a search results page is typically two or three paid links at the top followed by organic links and then two or three more paid links at the bottom of the page. The order in which the links appear is important: one study found that a link presented at the top of the page has a 36 percent average click-through rate, which then declines rapidly to 12 percent and 9 percent for the second and third links.[19] By the tenth result listed, the click-through rate has dropped to 2 percent.[20]

Advertisers bid on keywords so that links to their sites will be at or near the top of the page. Where an advertiser lands on a page is a function of two factors: Google's Quality Score (GQS) and the bid price. GQS is primarily determined by the expected click-through rate, ad relevance, and landing page experience.[21] The product of GQS and the bid price equals the Ad Rank, which determines ad placement.

For example, assume advertiser A bids $1 with a GQS of 10 while advertiser B bids $2 with a GQS of 1. Even though B's bid price is higher, the link to A will appear at the top. This is because A has an Ad Rank of 10 ($1 × 10) compared to B with an Ad Rank of 2 ($2 × 1). The price you pay to Google, however, is not the same as the price you bid. Instead, Google divides the Ad Rank of the advertiser whose link is below yours by your GQS. This is to further incentivize quality sites, as the rate you pay decreases as your GQS rises. In our example, A would pay $0.20 (B's Ad Rank of 2 divided by A's GQS of 10). B would pay based on dividing the Ad Rank of advertiser C, whose link would be displayed as the third result, by B's GQS of 1, and so on down the line.

Thus, Google Ads' auctions are basically a series of simultaneous Vickrey auctions in which you pay the cost of the ad beneath yours—the second price, adjusted for GQS. But because it is a Vickrey auction, advertisers do not need to concern themselves with what others bid. Rather, the optimal strategy is for advertisers to bid the highest amount that makes economic sense for them. In anything other than a Vickrey auction, advertisers would need to be constantly shading their bids. Given that auctions for a set of keywords occur multiple times per minute, it would be costly for advertisers to monitor and then readjust their bids in real time. Instead, advertisers can simply bid the full economic value of a given ad and get on with their business.

Another way to think about Google's Vickrey auctions is that they encourage cooperation much like in the prisoner's dilemma. Non-Vickrey auctions on the Google Ads platform would have higher transaction costs, requiring advertisers to continuously monitor an auction to decide how much to shade their bids. If an advertiser did not do this, then they would be at a significant disadvantage to other advertisers that do. By agreeing to hold a Vickrey auction, all advertisers save on monitoring costs, the equivalent of mutual cooperation.

Because Google Ads auctions are so fast and furious, Vickrey auctions are the optimal mechanism to set the price for search ads. Bidders do not have to be concerned with what other bidders are bidding or constantly monitor auctions. In a world of incomplete information and high monitoring costs, Vickrey auctions have real benefits.

eBay Auctions: Bid Last and Often

Vickrey-style auctions are also used by eBay. The winning bidder pays the second-highest bid plus a bid increment that varies with the price. For example, an item on eBay priced at $200 has a $2.50 bid increment.[22] However, there is one significant twist on eBay compared with other Vickrey auctions: the second-highest bid price plus the next bidding increment is publicly displayed.[23] This is because eBay enables the display of the second-highest bid through "proxy" bidding, in which bidders enter the maximum price they are willing to pay. However, eBay only displays the second-highest bid plus the appropriate bid increment.

For example, assume bidder A and bidder B initially submit maximum bids of $210 and $200, respectively, for an item. eBay will display a price of $202.50, the second-highest bid price of B plus the bid increment of $2.50. If B increases their bid to $220, then eBay will show a price of $212.50, the new second-highest bid price of A plus the bid increment. If nothing else changes, B wins the auction and pays $212.50.

A characteristic of most eBay auctions is a frenzy of bidding in the last minutes of the auction, known as "sniping." Unlike a standard Vickrey auction in which prices of the bidders are concealed, eBay auctions disclose the second-highest bid, and therefore there is an incentive to wait until the very last moment to disclose your bid to others. Studies have shown that sniping is typical for experienced users. But most people are infrequent users of eBay and simply enter their maximum bid price and then stop monitoring the auction.[24] In one survey, more than 90 percent of eBay users had not used snipe software, which automatically increases the maximum bid price in the last seconds of an eBay auction.[25]

Given that most eBay users are not frequent participants in auctions, the company was wise to employ a version of a Vickrey auction. The value of a ragged and faded T-shirt from an unknown rock band from the 1970s may be worth $100 to someone who attended every performance and $10 to a bidder who did not. A second-price auction in which proxy bidding hides the highest bid assures a bidder that they are not overpaying just because a piece of clothing brings back fond memories of a misspent youth.

The adoption of Vickrey auctions from the start was one reason eBay was able to attract more buyers compared with other competing auction sites that were based on traditional first-price auctions. eBay understood the power of network effects: the site with the most buyers will attract the most sellers, which becomes a virtuous circle. By employing Vickrey auctions, eBay was buyer friendly from day one.

Can't Wait so Buy It Now

When eBay first started, it was purely an auction site, known as AuctionWeb. Even today, most people think of eBay in terms of bidding on miscellaneous items. But in fact, most items on eBay are bought at a seller-determined fixed price or Buy It Now (BIN) price.[26] In that sense, eBay has become more like Amazon than an auction site.

BIN pricing was first introduced in November 2000, nearly five years after the first transaction on eBay, the purchase of a broken laser pointer still owned by the original buyer, Canadian Mark Fraser.[27] (I suspect this item will be offered on eBay someday at a price that far exceeds the original winning bid amount.) To use the BIN feature, sellers must set the BIN price 30 percent higher than an item's starting auction price, and the BIN price will disappear when someone bids higher than the reserve price. The BIN price can remain, however, if a bid does not reach at least 50 percent of the BIN price in four categories: motors, tickets, clothing, and cell phones.[28]

BIN pricing would seem to benefit only buyers, another example of eBay seeking to be a buyer-friendly site. Of course, when attempting to market large numbers of goods, a fixed price makes sense for buyer and seller. However, a seller of a single item using BIN pricing discloses up front the price at which they are willing to transact. If that price is lower than what could be achieved in a subsequent auction, then the seller has lost revenue. If the price is higher than what could be gained in a subsequent auction, then the seller has gained nothing. By listing a BIN price, the seller would seem to have only a downside.

However, BIN prices have proven to be quite successful for sellers on eBay. We know this because otherwise BIN pricing would not today constitute most eBay transactions.

Part of the reason BIN pricing is so popular is that it takes advantage of the differing degrees of impatience among bidders. Some bidders are willing to wait for the auction to play out over days to get the cheapest possible price. However, other bidders are not so patient, either because of higher opportunity costs or simply an urge for immediate gratification. By offering a BIN price, sellers can take advantage of an impatient bidder who shows up for an auction. In effect, sellers can charge a higher price for satisfying a need to have it now. If no impatient bidder arrives, then the auction proceeds as planned. Another reason BIN pricing is used for most transactions is that it exploits the differences between risk-averse and risk-seeking bidders. A risk-averse bidder will be willing to pay a BIN price now to guarantee winning the auction. The additional revenues from impatient and risk-averse bidders likely outweigh the instances in which a seller mistakenly underprices an item.

In fact, numerous experiments have shown that buyer impatience and risk aversion are real. It has been demonstrated that the longer the duration of an auction, the higher the revenues to a seller in an auction with a BIN price.[29]

Regardless of the type of auction, even the efficient and time-saving Vickrey auction, one issue is common to all: the winner knows they paid more than anybody else.

So winners often wonder—did I pay too much?

The Winner's Curse: Gain Nothing or Lose Something

The role of the winner's curse in auctions was first formally proposed in a paper titled "Competitive Bidding in High-Risk Situations," written in 1971 by three Atlantic Richfield petroleum engineers, Edward Capen, Robert Clapp, and William Campbell.[30] While the term "winner's curse" appears nowhere in this article, the idea runs throughout the paper.

Based on their experiences over many years of bidding on petroleum leases in the Gulf region of the southern United States, the engineers wrote that

> the "successful" bidders may have not been so successful after all . . . and the industry probably is not making as much return on its investment as intended. In fact, if one ignores the era before 1950, when land was a good deal cheaper, he finds that the Gulf has paid off at something less than the local credit union.[31]

The magnitude of the winner's curse can be measured in two ways. One metric measures the price paid against the actual value realized. The other metric compares the price paid to the estimated value before the auction took place. If the price paid is higher than the actual value, then the successful bidder suffers a loss. If the price paid is higher than the estimated value, then the buyer may still make money but nevertheless will be disappointed. In the cases of oil leases in the Gulf, the three engineers were arguing the latter: Atlantic Richfield and other oil companies made money, just not as much as they had expected.

A commonly referenced experiment to illustrate the winner's curse involves a glass jar full of coins and a lecture hall full of undergraduates. A professor offers students the opportunity to bid on the coins in the jar. When asked to estimate the total dollar value of the coins, a roomful of college students will offer a wide range of estimates, some too high and others too low. The average of all the bids will often approximate the true value. But the "winning" student, the highest bidder, always seems to lose money. This experiment has been repeated many times, at various universities, with the same result.

The person who guesses the highest dollar value of the coins in the jar is equivalent to the highest bidder in an auction. The conclusion from these experiments is that winning bidders typically pay too much.

The three Atlantic Richfield engineers wrote: "We would venture that many times when one purchases property it is because someone else has already looked at it and said, 'Nix.' The sober man must consider, 'Was he right? Or am I right?'"[32]

They concluded that the winner's curse was inherent in the auction process:

> *Even though each bidder estimates his value properly on average, he tends to win at the worst times—namely when he most over-estimates value. The error is not the fault of the explorationists. They are doing creditable work on a tough job. The problem is simply a quirk of the competitive bidding environment.*[33]

Based on the above, the logic of the winner's curse seems convincing and the evidence compelling. But if the winner of an auction almost always loses money, then why would anybody participate in an auction? It would seem that by participating in an auction, you either do not win and gain nothing or win and lose something.

The answer is nobody knowingly would participate if those were the only two potential outcomes. Consider the experiment with the jar full of coins and the college students. At some point, those students who consistently "won" would run out of money and stop bidding. Auctions in which the "winners" consistently lose money will eventually run out of bidders.

But the three Atlantic Richfield engineers did not claim in their seminal 1971 paper that oil companies had lost money on the oil leases that were awarded. Rather, they concluded that the oil leases were, on average, profitable—just not as profitable as the winning bidders had originally estimated. In this case, the winning bidders could continue to bid without running out of money, and therefore the winner's curse would not necessarily be self-correcting.

Common versus Private Value: I Own It and You Don't

The three engineers also did not consider the difference between common and private value. The common value of an asset is the value to anyone who owns it; the private value is the value to a specific individual or firm. In many cases, the common value is based on the bidder's expectation of the future resale price, whereas the private value is a function of the benefits to a particular buyer. In general, private values among bidders will vary more widely than common values. For example, a bottle of wine has private value for a wine drinker but a common value for a wine merchant. A wider range of values will probably be placed on a bottle of first-growth Bordeaux by wine drinkers than by knowledgeable beverage distributors.

In the 1971 article, the authors note that three large companies in particular—Phillips, Sunoco, and Texaco—seemed to consistently be victims of the winner's curse. As vertically integrated firms with refining and distribution operations, the three companies may have found it beneficial to secure exploration assets to feed the rest of their operations. By contrast, firms engaging only in exploration are driven by a goal of acquiring oil at the cheapest price for subsequent resale. It is possible that the vertically integrated oil firms attached a higher private value to securing the oil leases.

Unfortunately, at least for the purposes of our analysis, the Arab oil embargo caused the price of oil to increase dramatically after the award of the leases listed in the 1971 paper. As a result, it is difficult to analyze the true profitability of the oil leases to the winning bidders. A subsequent analysis of the oil leases cited in the article demonstrated that the average profit per tract was more than $2 million net of bidding and exploration costs.[34] Even Texaco, the largest and most vertically integrated of the bidders, had a positive return on its winning bids, earning on average $1.18 million per tract.[35] An analysis of whether this was an adequate rate of return on capital based on common value is not straightforward given the spike in oil prices after the auction. The same analysis based on private value to the winning bidders is even more complex, as determining the upstream strategic benefits to a vertically integrated firm of an assured supply of crude oil cannot be readily quantified by an outside observer. In my view, it is difficult to conclude definitively, even with the benefit of hindsight, that the oil companies overpaid.

In fact, the worth of most everything has varying degrees of private and common value. In art auctions, it is difficult to determine whether the winning bidder paid too much. The amount of pleasure from owning a particular painting, the private value, is likely to differ among individuals. Of course, there is still a component of common value in a painting if the owner wishes to sell it someday. Similarly, a wine drinker may later decide to part with an unopened bottle, or a wine merchant may opt to consume some of their own inventory. An additional part of private value can be the act of winning itself, which may have its own emotional rewards. Some may take great pleasure in besting a rival or excluding others from ownership.

One art critic is reported to have said:

> *After Michelangelo's pictures and the Medici porcelain, the rarest thing he had ever seen among collectors was goodwill, and he drew the conclusion that the collector's mania embraced the desire to own things for oneself . . . and the desire to stop other people from owning anything.*[36]

What appears to be the winner's curse may just be a difference in private values among bidders.

In the end, the solution proposed by the three Atlantic Richfield engineers was simple: everybody in the oil industry should bid less. But if the engineers had discovered a systemic inefficiency in the bidding process for oil leases, then the best course of action would have been to keep those insights confidential and profit from the knowledge. Given the conclusions of the paper, Atlantic Richfield should have withdrawn from submitting all but the lowest of bids and allowed its competitors to continue to overpay for leases. Instead, the three engineers published their findings and recommended the industry revise its bidding procedures to compensate for the winner's curse.

My speculation is that part of the motivation to disclose their findings was to encourage competitors to reduce their bids, allowing the oil industry to increase profits at the expense of leaseholders in subsequent auctions.

Further evidence that the winner's curse may not be as significant as some have argued is an auction that occurs most weekdays involving trillions of dollars.

The Stock Market: Winning All the Time

The owners of a stock are the winners of a daily auction that occurs on stock exchanges throughout the world. If the winner's curse was widespread in stock markets, then those fund managers subject to it would consistently underperform those who were not and soon would no longer be employed as fund managers. Given the demands of investors and the means to readily compare investment performance, the process of financial natural selection would quickly eliminate those victimized by the winner's curse. Thus, it seems improbable that the winner's curse could persist in financial markets.

But stock markets have two features that make these daily, real-time auctions less vulnerable to the winner's curse.

First, there are up-to-date prices for stocks. Because the price of a stock is disclosed before an order to purchase shares is submitted, the buyer is prevented from paying an amount much higher than what thousands of other investors very recently believed a company was worth. By contrast, there is no price history on a new oil well lease covering parts of the ocean floor beneath the Gulf of Mexico. In our example of coins in a jar, the unfortunate undergraduate who had the "winning" bid does not have the benefit of the experience of students in the previous classes. When a Picasso comes up for auction for the first time in fifty years, buyers have a lot less information about the value others place on the work of art.

Second, stocks can be shorted or sold by existing investors. If a stock's price is bid up too high, short sellers will borrow shares and then sell those shares into the market in anticipation of buying back the shares at a lower price. Alternatively, existing holders of a stock may also sell if the company becomes too highly valued. By contrast, there is no way to "short" a new, previously unawarded oil lease. Undergraduate students are not given the opportunity to bring in their own jars filled with coins once they realize that some of their fellow students will pay too much for various combinations of pennies, nickels, and dimes. The same with a Picasso. If the great Spanish artist were alive and he offered to recreate his masterpiece once a certain price was reached, this would limit the value of his paintings.

The winner's curse may be real but only in certain circumstances. Specifically, a lack of publicly disclosed recent prices and the inability of others to sell or sell short increase the risk that a bidder suffers from the winner's curse. Even then, overbidding should be corrected over time, as those who consistently underperform drop out of subsequent auctions. A constant stream of new, naïve bidders would be necessary, even in these circumstances, for the winner's curse to persist.

In my view, bidders do risk experiencing the winner's curse in auctions in which there are no publicly disclosed up-to-date prices and no opportunities for others to sell or sell short. And this risk is compounded when many new, naïve bidders are participating in the auction. When all three of these conditions are present, a potential buyer would probably be better off not investing the time and effort to bid at all. In these limited circumstances, winning the auction could very well be a losing proposition.

Turning the Winner's Curse on Its Head: Rigging Auctions

The winner's curse is not always a curse: sometimes it is a blessing. At least, it was for a while at Salomon Brothers.

From 1989 to 1991, the bond arbitrage group at Salomon Brothers was able to rig a number of auctions held by the US Department of the Treasury. In response, the Treasury changed how government securities were auctioned.

Prior to 1992, the Treasury sold securities in a sealed-bid first-price auction. The department accepted bids, the lowest yields first, until all securities were sold. The Treasury would typically issue strips of securities of varying maturities from three months to thirty years. The arbitrage group at Salomon figured out that they could corner the market on a particular strip of securities by outbidding everyone else. Once in control of the market for a particular Treasury security, Salomon could squeeze out other buyers, forcing them to pay an above-market price.

The Treasury was aware that a Wall Street firm could attempt to corner the market on a particular strip of securities and had in place a rule that no one firm could be awarded more than 35 percent of a given issue. To get around this prohibition, Salomon entered bids from its own account for 35 percent of an issue and submitted bids in the names of its institutional customers for the balance of the securities to be sold. However, these institutional customers were unaware that bids had been submitted on their behalf. In fact, the real buyer was Salomon itself. As a result, Salomon Brothers ended up owning 100 percent of several maturities.[37] Through this deception, Salomon was able to corner the market on billions of dollars of US government securities at auction.

After the Salomon Brothers scandal, the Treasury decided to reevaluate how securities were auctioned. In 1992, it switched from first-price to second-price auctions for several maturities. Later, in 1998, all Treasurys were switched to second-price auctions. In addition, a class of bids, known as noncompetitive bids, was introduced in which bidders submit an amount of a security they are willing to purchase. The actual purchase price is set by the market-clearing price, after adding up all the competitive and noncompetitive bids. In effect, a noncompetitive bid is no different than submitting an above-market bid in a second-price auction, guaranteeing that the bidder will pay the market-clearing price, whatever that may be.

One of the advantages of a second-price auction is that the market manipulation by bad actors is much more difficult. In Vickrey auctions of securities, such as those based on second-price and noncompetitive bids, participants are protected from short squeezes and many other forms of manipulation because all bidders can participate alongside the bad actors, as the second price determines the market-clearing yield. Once the US government switched to second-price auctions, the smart move for the traders who populated the bond arbitrage group at Salomon (and they were really smart, though not really honest) was to not try anything funny.

Although second-price auctions discourage market manipulation, most national treasuries of the world today auction government securities on a first-price basis. Among developed nations, thirty-three countries, such as France, Germany, and the United Kingdom, continue to use first-price auctions. Only nine countries, including Australia, Switzerland, and the United States, rely on second-price auctions.[38]

Stock Markets: Double Trouble for Investors

The US equity market and most stock markets around the world are examples of double auctions. In the examples above, we analyzed markets in which price was determined by buyers submitting bids to a seller. In the case of many stock markets, participants simultaneously offer to buy or sell a particular security at varying prices and in different amounts. When the price and amounts match, a trade is executed. In effect, two open first-price auctions are happening at once.

As with any first-price auction, buyers and sellers have an incentive to shade. This is particularly true given the vast amounts of monies that exchange hands in today's modern stock markets. In 2020, about $136 trillion worth of equities crossed the global stock exchanges.[39] The difference between the bid and ask prices varies by security. For the most liquid securities, the bid-offer spread can be as little as five basis points, or 0.05 percent.[40] For the many illiquid stocks, the spread between the buyer's and seller's prices can be more than 5 percent. Depending on how the data are weighted, estimates of the average spread for stocks can vary widely. However, most research has yielded estimates between 20 and 60 basis points.[41] Assuming the midpoint of those estimates, the annual value of the bid-offer spread on world equity markets is $544 billion ($137 trillion × 0.004). A financial firm able to capture even a portion of that spread would be quite profitable.

In fact, many hedge funds and securities houses do exploit investors and gain for themselves a portion of the more than half trillion dollars of bid-offer spread through payment for order flow, or PFOF.

To illustrate, assume the bid and offer prices for stock XYZ are $100 and $101, respectively, a spread of $1. A hedge fund pays a brokerage house a fee, let's say $0.10, for a sell order from one of the brokerage firm's investors. The hedge fund buys the stock at $100, the prevailing bid price, from the brokerage house's customer and immediately offers to pay another brokerage house $0.10 for a buy order. If successful, the hedge fund will then sell the shares to the other brokerage house's customer at $101, pocketing $0.80, or the $1 spread less two $0.10 fees paid for the respective buy and sell orders.

In an ideal world, the brokerage firms would not engage in PFOF. Instead, the brokerage firms representing the buyers and sellers would come down equally in price, agreeing to meet in the middle and transact at $100.50 for the mutual benefit of the investors. This would save the buyer and seller each $0.50. With PFOF, the $1 spread accrues to the hedge fund and brokerage house, which take for themselves $0.80 and $0.20, respectively.

For many brokerage firms, PFOF is a significant portion of their revenues. Robinhood is an online brokerage firm that went public in 2021 to much fanfare. Robinhood's website brags that the company offers "commission-free investing" that gives individuals a fair shot to invest in the stock market.[42] The company's CEO says that his mission is to "level the playing field for retail investors."[43] In the first quarter of 2021, 81 percent of Robinhood's revenues were from PFOF.[44]

In my opinion, the double first-price auctions that characterize the world's equity markets are the right pricing mechanisms for determining the value of public companies. However, PFOF directly transfers part of the savings of Main Street investors to Wall Street brokers and hedge fund operators. One way to limit this wealth transfer would be to reduce the frequency of the double auctions held for stocks.

Suppose auctions for stocks occurred only once daily. Investors could enter buy and sell orders, and at the end of the day all transactions would occur at a single price. To determine a market-clearing price, investors could enter bids and offers of varying amounts that would be fully disclosed throughout the day. In our example, the buyer and seller could each enter orders at $100.50. In a once-a-day auction, investors would no longer pay the bid-offer spread to hedge funds or brokerage houses.

Of course, Wall Street would not welcome such a system. Besides putting many hedge funds and brokerage houses out of business, it would also largely eliminate the need for most of the employees of the major stock exchanges. Continuous trading generates significant profits for those on Wall Street, monies that come directly out of the pockets of retail and institutional investors. There is a reason the financial services industry mints so many billionaires.

Continuous trading largely benefits those in the trading business. In my opinion, it would be better to have the more than half a trillion dollars each year in equity market bid-offer spreads remain in the retirement and pension funds of Main Street investors rather than lining the pockets of Wall Street traders.

Conclusions

In an idealized world, all four types of auctions will yield the same results. In the real world, we have seen how risk-averse buyers will pay more, while risk-seeking buyers will pay less. We have shown that a reserve price effectively adds another informed buyer to the benefit of the seller. Given incomplete information, bidders in open first-price, sealed first-price, and open second-price auctions will shade their bids, reducing the revenues to sellers.

But in sealed second-price auctions, or Vickrey auctions, buyers have an incentive to bid the full economic value. And Vickrey auctions have the added benefit of cutting monitoring costs. The real-world advantages of Vickrey auctions are apparent at Google and eBay. It is not clear why these advantages are not apparent to many governments. The potential for market manipulation with first-price auctions is real in financial markets, and yet, even after the Salomon Brothers scandal, many countries continue to sell government securities through first-price auctions. We also saw how hedge funds and brokerage firms siphon off billions of dollars from pension and retirement funds each year, exploiting the double first-price auctions that characterize stock markets around the world.

Fortunately, the winner's curse may not be as prevalent as many believe. For starters, differences between private and common value probably explain many of the alleged examples of the winner's curse. Ultimately, the winner's curse should be self-correcting, as there are only so many auctions that buyers are willing to lose by winning. Nevertheless, you should be more cautious when bidding in auctions without readily available recent prices or the ability for existing holders to sell and others to short an item.

William Vickrey was awarded the Nobel Prize for his application of game theory to auctions. So he knew a thing or two about how best to set prices. That is why he spent a good part of his life advocating for greater use of the type of auction that bears his name.

He was right.

Epilogue

WE HAVE SEEN HOW GAME theory has applications far beyond poker, chess, or checkers. It shows us when to cooperate or compete. It informs us on when to fight or sue for peace. It demonstrates how to structure incentives to achieve better outcomes. With a knowledge of game theory, we are less likely to be outplayed by others.

We have demonstrated that the optimal strategy for an iterated game is fundamentally different from a game played once. In the prisoner's dilemma, defection is the best strategy in a one-off game. But over multiple rounds, Tit-for-Tat is more effective, by rewarding cooperation and punishing defection. When employing a Tit-for-Tat strategy, it is important to be nice and cooperate on the first interaction with others. But it is also critical to retaliate and return any defection in like measure. If we want to encourage cooperation, then we must strike back, an-eye-for-an-eye instead of turning the other cheek. In other words, the best strategy is decidedly Old Testament. The only caveat to the above is that we should only retaliate once, and then we should be forgiving and move on as if the defection never happened. In all cases, we need to be clear. If our strategy is not understood by others, then they will question whether cooperation will be consistently rewarded.

In the animal kingdom, the equivalent of Tit-for-Tat can evolve, in the form of an evolutionarily stable strategy. However, this occurs with less frequency since encounters between "hawks" and "doves" often have asymmetrical payoffs, including death. In addition, it is often difficult to identify whether the opponent is a relative or has been encountered previously. By contrast, game theory is more applicable to the battle of the sexes in humans. The fundamental differences between males and females—the size and number of sex cells, internal versus external fertilization, and paternity—are the sources of the conflict over who is "left holding the baby." Unfortunately, human males are better at competing than caring. Despite this, *Homo sapiens* are today mostly a monogamous species. But monogamy may not last, as the conditions on the ground in the battle of the sexes have changed.

We have discussed the madness of mutual assured destruction, or MAD, a classic case of the prisoner's dilemma, in which nations threaten to commit mass suicide to stop mass murder. The fundamental assumption behind MAD—the automatic launch of a second full-scale nuclear strike—is highly questionable, both for moral and utilitarian reasons. In addition, we now better understand the science around nuclear winter and that a second strike is likely to do more harm than good. Consequently, I have argued that the current stockpile of more than eleven thousand warheads maintained by the United States and Russia is unnecessary and reckless. Some number less than one thousand for each nation is more than enough.

We have analyzed all-pay auctions, which are common in encounters between individuals and groups. In World War I, the costs from battle far exceeded the gains from victory. We learned about pure and mixed strategies and when to use them. We also saw how a strong central authority provides the overwhelming force to stop wars of attrition within a community.

We explored the development of new voting systems. While Arrow's impossibility theorem proves there is no perfect election mechanism, instant runoff voting is less vulnerable to spoilers and spoilers-as-winners. In addition, this voting system is not subject to cycling—issues that plague ranked-choice, approval, and score voting. But any of the above are better than plurality voting, which is regularly employed around the globe for selecting political candidates and policies.

We have proven that in an idealized world all four basic types of auctions yield the same outcomes. However, in the real world, Vickrey auctions should eliminate shading. Furthermore, the winner's curse is not as prevalent as most believe and ultimately should be self-correcting. Nevertheless, you should be careful when bidding in an auction in which others cannot sell or short the same item and there are no recent prices.

This book began with a description of a doomsday device called Perimeter. This Soviet-era automated defense system, which is still operational today, is a consequence of the current nuclear prisoner's dilemma being played out between the United States and Russia. Both nations are acting in their own perceived self-interest, and as a result, both nations (and the rest of the world) are worse off. Similarly, we have seen that in conventional wars, elections, and financial markets, the gains to a few are often more than offset by the losses to the many.

Game theory shows us that the interests of individuals and nations are frequently not aligned. But asking individuals and nations to abandon self-interest is not a practical solution. Instead, we should learn the lessons that game theory has taught us and find ways to incentivize others to fight less and cooperate more for the collective good.

Game theory has given us the tools to build a better world. We should pick up those tools and get to work.

Acknowledgments

I AM FORTUNATE THAT STEWART Ethier agreed to work with me on this book. I gained tremendously from his insights and constructive criticism. In addition to his former day job as a professor of mathematics, Stewart has written several books and numerous articles on game theory, particularly related to gambling. I highly recommend them. Particularly if you want to win.

Gary Williams has been a great friend and mentor and, as in my previous book, offered advice on the front and back covers and everything in between. His comments on the text changed my thinking in many places. Two good friends who are active in politics critiqued the chapter on elections. Given the prominence of their positions, I will not name them here, since in today's poisoned politics, anything can be used against anyone. But you know who you are.

The team at Greenleaf was terrific as usual. Justin Branch, Tyler LeBleu, and Chase Quarterman all did excellent work. Sally Garland once again deftly shepherded the writer through the process of turning a manuscript into a book. Her work on permissions went above and beyond. Judy Marchman meticulously copyedited the manuscript with an accuracy worthy of the most skilled marksman. Her comments were always on target. Kirstin Andrews obsessively proofed the final edit down to the last comma. I especially want to thank Heather Settler, whom I consider a collaborator as much as a developmental editor. Just as with my previous book, Heather forced me to reconsider and restate many parts of the manuscript. She is responsible for none of the mistakes and most of the clarity.

To my family—I could not have completed this book without your support and patience. In our house, the words *family means everything* are often said and remain forever true. This book is dedicated to you.

References

Abdi, Farshid, and Angelo Ranaldo. 2017. "A Simple Estimation of Bid-Ask Spreads from Daily Close, High, and Low Prices." *The Review of Financial Studies* 30, no. 12 (December): 4437–80. https://doi.org/10.1093/rfs/hhx084.

Abella, Alex. 2008. *Soldiers of Reason*. New York: Harcourt Inc.

Anderton, Charles H., and John R. Carter. 2019. *Principles of Conflict Economics*. Cambridge: Cambridge University Press.

Arney, Kat. 2021. "Everything You Ever Wanted to Know about the Evolution of Sex (But Were Too Afraid to Ask)." *The Genetics Society Podcast*, August 15, 2021. https://geneticsunzipped.com/news/2019/8/15/evolution-of-sex.

Arrow, Kenneth. 1948. "The Possibility of a Universal Social Welfare Function." RAND Corporation. September 28, 1948. https://www.rand.org/pubs/papers/P41.html.

Arrow, Kenneth. (1951) 1970. *Social Choice and Individual Values*. 2nd ed. New Haven, CT: Yale University Press.

Axelrod, Robert. 1984. *The Evolution of Cooperation*. New York: Perseus Books.

Axelrod, Robert. 1997. *The Complexity of Cooperation*. Princeton, NJ: Princeton University Press.

Axelrod, Robert, and Michael D. Cohen. 1999. *Harnessing Complexity*. New York: The Free Press.

Banks, Eric. 2004. *The Failure of Wall Street*. New York: St. Martin's Press.

Barbuti, Roberto, Selma Mautner, Giorgio Carnevale, Paolo Milazzo, Aureliano Rama, and Christian Sturmbauer. 2012. "Population Dynamics with a Mixed Type of Sexual and Asexual Reproduction in a Fluctuating Environment." *BMC Evolutionary Biology* 12, no. 49: 40. doi: https://dx.doi.org/10.1186%2F1471-2148-12-49.

Beyer, Vicki L. 1992. "The Legacy of the Shoup Mission: Taxation Inequities and Tax Reform in Japan." *UCLA Pacific Basin Law Journal* 10, no. 2. doi: 10.5070/P8102021998.

Binmore, Ken. 2007. *Game Theory.* Oxford: Oxford University Press.

Bracken, Paul. 2012. *The Second Nuclear Age.* New York: St. Martin's.

Brasch, Sam. 2020. "A Colorado Professor Is Warning the World of Nuclear Winter—Again." CPR News, January 9, 2020. https://www.cpr.org/2020/01/09/a-colorado-professor-is-warning-the-world-of-nuclear-winter-again.

Brenner, Menachem, Dan Galai, and Orly Sade. 2007. "Auctioning Sovereign Bonds: A Global Cross-Section Investigation of the Price Mechanism." https://www.bauer.uh.edu/nlangberg/Finance%20Seminar/SADE_countries_bidders_choice_November_21_2007-clean.pdf.

Bruce-Briggs, B. 2000. *Supergenius: The Mega-Worlds of Herman Kahn.* New York: North American Policy Press.

Buss, David. 2021. *When Men Behave Badly.* New York: Little, Brown Spark.

Capen, E. C., R. V. Clapp, and W. M. Campbell. 1971. "Competitive Bidding in High-Risk Situations." *Journal of Petroleum Technology* 23 (June): 641–563. https://www.cs.princeton.edu/courses/archive/spr09/cos444/papers/capen_et_al71.pdf.

Carroll, Lewis. 1871. *Through the Looking-Glass.* Electronic version available online through the Sabian Assembly. https://sabian.org/looking_glass1.php.

Charlesworth, Brian. 2004. "John Maynard Smith." *Genetics* 168, no. 3 (November): 1105–1109. https://www.ncbi.nlm.nih.gov/pmc/articles/PMC1448785.

Chatterjee, Krishnendu, Johannes G. Reiter, and Martin A. Nowak. 2012. "Evolutionary Dynamics of Biological Auctions." *Theoretical Population Biology* 81, no. 1: 69–80. https://www.ncbi.nlm.nih.gov/pmc/articles/PMC3279759/.

Chen, Janet, Su-I Lu, and Dan Vekhter. 2021. "Von Neumann and the Development of Game Theory," in *Game Theory*. https://cs.stanford.edu/people/eroberts/courses/soco/projects/1998-99/game-theory/neumann.html.

Columbia University Record. 1997. "William Vickrey (1914–1996): Vickrey One Year Later: Catching Up with a Thinker Way Ahead of His Time." *Columbia University Record*, October 10, 1997. https://econ.columbia.edu/faculty/in-memoriam/william-vickrey-1914-1996.

Cooper, Alexandra, and Michael C. Munger. 2000. "The (Un)Predictability of Primaries with Many Candidates: Simulation Evidence." *Public Choice* 103, no. 3/4: 337–355. https://www.jstor.org/stable/pdf/30026328?refreqid=fastly-default%3A62e3191f518b6b453634f16d310d42fc.

Csillag, Ron. 2007. "Anatol Rapoport, Academic: 1911–2007." *The Globe and Mail*, January 31, 2007. https://www.theglobeandmail.com/incoming/anatol-rapoport-academic-1911-2007/article17990140/.

Davenport, Kelsey, and Kingston Reif. 2020. "Nuclear Weapons: Who Has What at a Glance." Arms Control Association, August 2020. https://www.armscontrol.org/factsheets/Nuclearweaponswhohaswhat.

Davis, Morton. 1983. *Game Theory*. Mineola, NY: Dover Publications.

Dawkins, Richard. 1976. *The Selfish Gene*. Oxford: Oxford University Press.

Dawkins, Richard. 1986. *The Blind Watchmaker*. New York: W.W. Norton.

Diamond, Jed. 2020. "The Evolution of Sex: Why Men and Women Are the Way They Are." *The Willits News*, August 17, 2020. https://www.willitsnews.com/2020/08/17/the-evolution-of-sex-why-men-and-women-are-the-way-they-are.

Dieter, Irene. 2003. "Dispelling the Myth of Election 2000: Did Nader Cost Gore the Election?" City of Alameda Greens, May 2003. http://www.cagreens.org/alameda/city/0803myth/myth.html.

Dixit, Avinash, and Barry J. Nalebuff. 1993. *The Art of Strategy*. New York: W.W. Norton.

Douglas-Fairhurst, Robert. 2015. *The Story of Alice*. Cambridge, MA: Harvard University Press.

Downing, Sam. 2015. "Animals That Don't Have Penises (and the Strange Replacements They Have Instead)." Entertainment, nine.com.au. https://www.nine.com.au/entertainment/viral/animals-that-don-t-have-penises/fd93fe3e-2b29-48f7-9290-b02437586c34.

Drèze, Jacques H. 1998. "William S. Vickrey," in *Biographical Memoirs*. Vol. 75. National Academy of Sciences of the United States of America. Washington, DC: National Academy Press. https://www.nap.edu/read/9649/chapter/21.

Dummies. 2016. "How eBay's Buy It Now Option Works." Updated March 26, 2016. https://www.dummies.com/business/online-business/ebay/how-ebays-buy-it-now-option-works.

Dunbar, Robin. 1998. *Grooming, Gossip and the Evolution of Language*. Cambridge, MA: Harvard University Press.

Dunham, Will. 2014. "Infanticide Common among Adult Males in Many Mammal Species." Reuters: Environment, November 13, 2014. https://www.reuters.com/article/us-science-infanticide/infanticide-common-among-adult-males-in-many-mammal-species-idUSKCN0IX2BA20141113.

Earth Institute at Columbia University. 2020. "Even a Limited India-Pakistan Nuclear War Would Bring Global Famine, Says Study: Soot from Firestorms Would Reduce Crop Production for Years." *ScienceDaily*, March 16, 2020. www.sciencedaily.com/releases/2020/03/200316152211.htm.

eBay. 2018. "If You Place a 'High Bid' Amount, and No One Else Bids Up to That, What Do You Owe?" eBay Buying Q&A, July 27, 2018. https://community.ebay.com/t5/Buying-Q-A/If-you-place-a-quot-high-bid-quot-amount-and-no-one-else-bids-up/qaq-p/28786219.

eBay. 2021a. "Listing Durations and Timings." eBay Customer Service, accessed September 28, 2021. https://www.ebay.com/help/selling/listings/ selecting-listing-duration?id=4652.

eBay. 2021b. "Our History." Accessed September 28, 2021. https://www .ebayinc.com/company/our-history.

eCommerce Bytes. 2017. "What Percentage of eBay Sales Are Auctions?" eCommerce Bytes (blog), December 1, 2017. https://www.ecommercebytes .com/C/letters/blog.pl?/pl/2017/12/1512179179.html.

Ellsberg, Daniel. 2017. *The Doomsday Machine*. New York: Bloomsbury Publishing.

Engelstädter, Jan. 2017. "Asexual but Not Clonal: Evolutionary Processes in Automictic Populations." *Genetics* 206, no. 2: 993–1009. https:// doi.org/10.1534/genetics.116.196873.

Enss, Chris. 2015. "Getting Personal on the Frontier: Mail-Order Brides." HistoryNet, February 2015. https://www.historynet.com/getting-personal -on-the-frontier-mail-order-brides.htm.

Farnam Street Media. 2017. "Attrition Warfare: When Even Winners Lose." fs.blog, accessed September 28, 2021. https://fs.blog/2017/07/ attrition-warfare.

Fine, Leslie R. 2021. "Auctions." Collection: The Economics of Special Markets. The Library of Economics and Liberty. https://www.econlib.org/ library/Enc/Auctions.html.

Flood, Merrill. 1952. *Some Experimental Games*. Revised June 1952. Santa Monica, CA: RAND Corporation.

Foley, Duncan. 2006. *Adam's Fallacy: A Guide to Economic Theology*. Cambridge, MA: Harvard University Press.

Freedman, Lawrence. 2013. *Strategy: A History*. Oxford: Oxford University Press.

Freedman, Lawrence, and Jeffrey Michaels. 2019. *The Evolution of Nuclear Strategy*. 4th ed. London: Palgrave Macmillan.

Frey, William. 2018. *Diversity Explosion*. Washington, DC: Brookings Institution.

Furness, Andrew I., and Isabella Capellini. 2019. "The Evolution of Parental Care Diversity in Amphibians." *Nature Communications* 10, no. 4709. https://doi.org/10.1038/s41467-019-12608-5.

Futter, Andrew. 2018. *Hacking the Bomb: Cyber Threats and Nuclear Weapons*. Washington, DC: Georgetown University Press.

Gardner, Roy. 2003. *Games for Business and Economics*. New York: John Wiley & Sons, Inc.

Gavin, Francis. 2020. *Nuclear Weapons and American Grand Strategy*. Washington, DC: The Brookings Institution.

Geary, David. 2021. *Male, Female: The Evolution of Human Sex Differences*. 3rd ed. Washington, DC: American Psychological Association.

Goodstein, David. 1998. "Mathematics to Madness, and Back." *The New York Times*, June 11, 1998. https://archive.nytimes.com/www.nytimes.com/books/98/06/07/daily/mind-book-review.html.

Google. 2021. "About Quality Score." Google Ads Help, September 28, 2021. https://support.google.com/google-ads/answer/6167118?hl=en.

Grady, John. 2021. "Russian and Chinese Nuclear Threats Pose Problem for U.S. Deterrence, Experts Say." *USNI News*, April 8, 2021. https://news.usni.org/2021/04/08/russian-and-chinese-nuclear-threats-pose-problem-for-u-s-deterrence-experts-say.

Greenfeld, Lawrence A., and Tracy L. Snell. 1999. "Women Offenders." Bureau of Justice Statistics Special Report, December 1999. https://bjs.ojp.gov/content/pub/pdf/wo.pdf.

Greenwood, P. J., P. H. Harvey, and M. Slatkin, eds. 1985. *Evolution: Essays in Honor of John Maynard Smith*. Cambridge: Cambridge University Press.

Gross, Rachel E. 2015. "A Peacock Must Be More Than Glorious." Slate, August 17, 2015. https://slate.com/technology/2015/08/peacock-evolution-through-sexual-selection-feathers-sounds-eye-tracking-and-lekking.html.

Harper, David. 2004. "John Maynard Smith: Leading Evolutionary Biologist, Keen to Make His Ideas Understood." *The Guardian*, April 21, 2004. https://www.theguardian.com/news/2004/apr/22/guardianobituaries .highereducation.

Hart, B., and H. Liddell. (1954) 1991. *Strategy*. New York: Penguin Group.

Henshaw, Jonathan M., Lutz Fromhage, and Adam G. Jones. 2019. "Sex Roles and the Evolution of Parental Care Specialization." *Proceedings of the Royal Society B: Biological Sciences*, August 28, 2019. https://doi.org/10.1098/ rspb.2019.1312.

Herron, Michael C., and Jeffrey B. Lewis. 2006. "Did Ralph Nader Spoil a Gore Presidency? Ballot-Level Study of Green and Reform Party Voters in the 2000 Presidential Election." https://www.sscnet.ucla.edu/polisci/faculty/ lewis/pdf/greenreform9.pdf.

Hodge, Jonathan K., and Richard E. Klima. 2018. *The Mathematics of Voting and Elections*. 2nd ed. Providence, RI: The American Mathematical Society.

Hoffman, David. 2009. *The Dead Hand: The Untold Story of the Cold War Arms Race and Its Dangerous Legacy*. Toronto: Doubleday.

Holt, Charles A., and Alvin E. Roth. 2004. "The Nash Equilibrium: A Perspective." *Proceedings of the National Academy of Sciences of the United States of America* 101, no. 12: 3999–4002. https://www.pnas.org/ content/101/12/3999.

Hotelling, Harold. 1929. "Stability in Competition." *The Economic Journal* 39, no. 153: 41–57. https://www.tcd.ie/Economics/staff/ppwalsh/papers/ Hotelling.pdf.

Hubbard, Timothy P., and Harry J. Paarsch. 2015. *Auctions*. Cambridge, MA: MIT Press.

Humanist News. 2001. John Maynard Smith. Humanists UK, *Humanist News* interview, Autumn 2001. https://humanism.org.uk/humanism/ the-humanist-tradition/20th-century-humanism/john-maynard-smith.

Hume, David. 1740. *A Treatise of Human Nature*. Oxford: Clarendon Press. Reprinted from the original edition in three volumes and edited, with an analytical index, by L. A. Selby-Bigge. https://oll.libertyfund.org/title/ bigge-a-treatise-of-human-nature#lf0213_head_001.

Hunt, Elle. 2017. "A Peacock's Tail: How Darwin Arrived at His Theory of Sexual Selection." *The Guardian*, May 19, 2017. https://www .theguardian.com/science/2017/may/19/a-peacocks-tail-how-darwin -arrived-at-his-theory-of-sexual-selection.

ICAN. 2019. "Enough is Enough: Global Nuclear Weapons Spending 2019." ICAN. https://www.icanw.org/report_73_billion_nuclear_weapons_ spending_2020.

Jervis, Robert. 2002. "Mutual Assured Destruction." *Foreign Policy* 133 (Nov.–Dec.): 40–42. https://www.jstor.org/stable/ 3183553?seq=1#metadata_info_tab_contents.

Kagel, John, and Dan Levin. 2002. *Common Value Auctions and the Winner's Curse*. Princeton, NJ: Princeton University Press.

Kahn, Herman. 1960a. "The Nature and Feasibility of War and Deterrence." Santa Monica, CA: The RAND Corporation.

Kahn, Herman. 1960b. *On Thermonuclear War*. Princeton, NJ: Princeton University Press.

Kahn, Herman. 1965. *On Escalation*. New York: Praeger.

Kahn, Herman. 1976. *The Next 200 Years*. New York: The Hudson Institute.

Kahn, Herman. 1984. *Thinking about the Unthinkable in the 1980s*. New York: The Hudson Institute.

Kaplan, Fred. 1983. *The Wizards of Armageddon*. New York: Simon & Schuster.

Kaplan, Fred. 2004. "Truth Stranger Than 'Strangelove.'" *The New York Times*, October 10, 2004. https://www.nytimes.com/2004/10/10/movies/ truth-stranger-than-strangelove.html.

Keeley, Lawrence. 1996. *War before Civilization*. Oxford: Oxford University Press.

Keller, Bill. 2013. "Rethinking the Unthinkable." *The New York Times*, January 11, 2013. https://www.nytimes.com/1981/03/15/magazine/rethinking-the-unthinkable.html.

Kennedy, Maev. 2001. "Alice Liddell's Archive Up for Auction." *The Guardian*, March 23, 2001. https://www.theguardian.com/uk/2001/mar/23/books.highereducation.

Khan Academy. 2021. "Embryology: Egg Meets Sperm." Khan Academy, accessed September 26, 2021. https://www.khanacademy.org/test-prep/mcat/cells/embryology/a/egg-meets-sperm.

Knifton, John. 2020. "Alice in Wonderland (4)." John Knifton (blog), August 22, 2020. https://johnknifton.com/tag/lorina-liddell.

Kopelman, Shirli. 2020. "Tit for Tat and Beyond: The Legendary Work of Anatol Rapoport." *Negotiation and Conflict Management Research* 13, no. 1: 60–84. https://doi.org/10.1111/ncmr.12172.

Krepinevich, Andrew, and Barry Watts. 2015. *The Last Warrior*. New York: Basic Books.

Kristensen, Hans M., and Matt Korda. 2021. "United States Nuclear Weapons, 2021." *Bulletin of the Atomic Scientists* 77, no. 1: 43–63. doi.org/10.1080/00963402.2020.1859865.

Kurrild-Klitgaard, Peter. 2016. "Trump, Condorcet and Borda: Voting Paradoxes in the 2016 Republican Presidential Primaries." Munich Personal RePEc Archive, MPRA Paper No. 75598, December 15, 2016. https://mpra.ub.uni-muenchen.de/75598/1/MPRA_paper_75598.pdf.

Kwon, Ha-Kyung. 2010. "Nash GS '50: 'The Phantom of Fine Hall.'" *The Daily Princetonian*, December 10, 2010. https://web.archive.org/web/20140506091547/http://dailyprincetonian.com/news/2010/12/nash-gs-50-the-phantom-of-fine-hall.

Leach, Karoline. 1996. "The Liddell Riddle." Extracted from article in the *Times Literary Supplement*, May 3, 1996. https://www.alice-in-wonderland .net/resources/analysis/interpretive-essays/the-liddell-riddle.

Leach, Karoline. 2005. "Who Mutilated Lewis Carroll's Diaries?" https://contrariwise.info/articles/WhoMutilatedCarrollsDiaries.pdf.

Leach, Karoline. 2015. *The Myth and Reality of Lewis Carroll*. London: Peter Owen.

LeBlanc, Steven. 2003. *Constant Battles—Why We Fight*. New York: St. Martin's Press.

Lehtonen, Jussi. 2017. "Gamete Size." *Encyclopedia of Evolutionary Psychological Science,* August 8, 2017. https://doi.org/ 10.1007/978-3-319-16999-6_3063-1.

Lewis, Meredith. 2011. "The Prisoner's Dilemma Posed by Free Trade Agreements." *Chicago Journal of International Law* 11, no. 2: Article 24.

Lieber, Keir, and Daryl G. Press. 2020. *The Myth of the Nuclear Revolution*. Ithaca, NY: Cornell University Press.

Lin, Ying. 2021. "10 eBay Statistics You Need to Know in 2021." Oberlo (blog), June 20, 2021. https://www.oberlo.com/blog/ebay-statistics.

Lissner, Will. 1946. "Mathematical Theory of Poker Is Applied to Business Problems." *The New York Times*, March 10, 1946. https://www.nytimes .com/1946/03/10/archives/mathematical-theory-of-poker-is-applied-to -business-problems-gamng.html.

Macaulay, Stewart. 1963. "Non-Contractual Relations in Business." *American Sociological Review* 28, no. 1: 55–67.

Macrae, Norman. 1992. *John von Neumann*. New York: Pantheon Books.

Maskin, Eric, and Amartya Sen. 2014. *The Arrow Impossibility Theorem*. New York: Columbia University.

Maynard Smith, John. (1958) 1975. *The Theory of Evolution*. Cambridge: Cambridge University Press.

Maynard Smith, John. 1978. *The Evolution of Sex*. Cambridge: Cambridge University Press.

Maynard Smith, John. 1982. *Evolution and the Theory of Games*. Cambridge: Cambridge University Press.

McCormick, Kristen. 2021. "10+ Free Ways to Get on the First Page of Google." WordStream (blog), June 5, 2021. https://www.wordstream.com/blog/ws/2020/08/19/get-on-first-page-google.

McKenna, Phil. 2008. "Vote of No Confidence." *New Scientist*, April 12, 2008, 30–33. Reproduced at https://rangevoting.org/McKennaText.

McLean, Iain, Alistair McMillan, and Burt L. Monroe. 1996. *A Mathematical Approach to Proportional Representation: Duncan Black on Lewis Carroll*. New York: Springer Science.

Menand, Louis. 2005. "Fat Man." *The New Yorker*, June 19, 2005. https://www.newyorker.com/magazine/2005/06/27/fat-man.

Merriam-Webster. 2021. "Sex." Merriam-Webster.com, accessed September 26, 2021. https://www.merriam-webster.com/dictionary/sex.

Mestel, Rosie. 2004. "John Maynard Smith, 84; Applied Game Theory to Evolution, Asked Why Animals Developed Sex." *Los Angeles Times*, April 24, 2004. https://www.latimes.com/archives/la-xpm-2004-apr-24-me-maynardsmith24-story.html.

Milgrom, Paul. 2017. *Discovering Prices*. New York: Columbia University Press.

Morgenstern, Oskar. 1976. "The Collaboration Between Oskar Morgenstern and John von Neumann on the Theory of Games." *Journal of Economic Literature* 14, no. 3: 805–816. https://www.jstor.org/stable/pdf/2722628?refreqid=fastly-default%3A17eab761aa6e38c8ca3449f0364cd9bd.

Moscow Times. 2018. "UN Predicts Falling Population, Rising Urbanization in Russia Through 2050." *The Moscow Times*, May 17, 2018. https://www.themoscowtimes.com/2018/05/17/un-predicts-falling-population-rising-urbanization-russia-through-2050-a61480.

Myerson, Roger B. 1999. "Nash Equilibrium and the History of Economic Theory." *Journal of Economic Literature* 36: 1067–1082. http://home .uchicago.edu/rmyerson/research/jelnash.pdf.

Nasar, Sylvia. 2011. *A Beautiful Mind.* New York: Simon & Schuster.

Nash, John F. Jr. 2021. "Biographical." NobelPrize.org. Nobel Prize Outreach AB 2021, accessed September 26, 2021. https://www.nobelprize.org/prizes/ economic-sciences/1994/nash/facts.

National Archives. 2021. "2020 Electoral College Results." Last updated April 16, 2021. https://www.archives.gov/electoral-college/2020.

National Conference of State Legislatures. 2020. "Debating the Electoral College." March 24, 2020. https://www.ncsl.org/research/elections-and -campaigns/debating-the-electoral-college.aspx.

Nee, Sean. 2004. "Professor John Maynard Smith 1920–2004." *Trends in Ecology & Evolution* 19, no. 7: 345–346. https://doi.org/10.1016/ j.tree.2004.05.007.

Nicas, Jack. 2017. "How Google's Ad Auctions Work." *The Wall Street Journal,* January 19, 2017. https://www.wsj.com/articles/how-googles -ad-auctions-work-1484827203.

Niou, Emerson M. S., and Peter C. Ordeshook. 1994. "A Game-Theoretic Interpretation of Sun Tzu's *The Art of War.*" *Journal of Peace Research* 31, no. 2: 161–174.

Nisan, Noam. 2012. "John Nash's Letter to the NSA." Turing's Invisible Hand: Computation, Economics, and Game Theory (blog), February 17, 2012. https://agtb.wordpress.com/2012/02/17/john-nashs-letter-to-the-nsa.

Norman, Geoffrey. 2007. "Field Marshal Sir Douglas Haig: World War I's Worst General." HistoryNet, June 2007. https://www.historynet.com/ field-marshal-sir-douglas-haig-world-war-is-worst-general.htm.

O'Connor, J. J., and E. F. Robertson. 2010. "Albert William Tucker." School of Mathematics and Statistics, University of St. Andrews, Scotland. https:// mathshistory.st-andrews.ac.uk/Biographies/Tucker_Albert.

Osipovich, Alexander. 2021. "Robinhood's Debut Is Clouded by SEC Scrutiny of Payment for Order Flow." *The Wall Street Journal*, July 7, 2021. https://www.wsj.com/articles/robinhoods-debut-is-clouded-by-sec-scrutiny-of-payment-for-order-flow-11625655600.

PBS. 2021. "The Advantage of Sex." Evolution Library, PBS.org, accessed September 26, 2021. https://www.pbs.org/wgbh/evolution/sex/advantage/page03.html.

Peterson, Martin. 2015. *The Prisoner's Dilemma*. Cambridge: Cambridge University Press.

Pinker, Steven. 2012. *The Better Angels of Our Nature*. New York: Penguin Books.

Poundstone, William. 1992. *Prisoner's Dilemma*. New York: Anchor Books.

Poundstone, William. 2008. *Gaming the Vote*. New York: Hill and Wang.

Prescott, Cynthia Culver. 2007. "'Why She Didn't Marry Him': Love, Power, and Marital Choice on the Far Western Frontier." *Western Historical Quarterly* 38, no. 1: 25–45. https://www.jstor.org/stable/25443458.

Quinn, Shannon. 2018. "10 Controversial Facts behind the Real Alice in Wonderland." History Collection, May 30, 2018. https://historycollection.com/10-controversial-facts-behind-the-real-alice-in-wonderland.

Quote Investigator. 2012. "Aeroplanes and Tanks Are Only Accessories to the Man and the Horse." November 30, 2012. https://quoteinvestigator.com/2012/11/30/horse-in-war.

Rapoport, Amnon, Darryl A. Seale, and Andrew M. Colman. 2015. "Is Tit-for-Tat the Answer?" *PLOS ONE*, July 30, 2015. https://doi.org/10.1371/journal.pone.0134128.

Rapoport, Anatol. 1960. *Fights, Games, and Debates*. Ann Arbor: University of Michigan Press.

Rapoport, Anatol. 1966. *Two-Person Game Theory*. Ann Arbor: University of Michigan Press.

Rapoport, Anatol. 1969. *Strategy and Conscience*. Ann Arbor: University of Michigan Press.

Rapoport, Anatol. 1970. *N-Person Game Theory*. Ann Arbor: University of Michigan Press.

Rapoport, Anatol. 1971. *The Big Two*. New York: Pegasus Books.

Rapoport, Anatol. 1992. *Peace: An Idea Whose Time Has Come*. Ann Arbor: University of Michigan Press.

Rapoport, Anatol. 2000. *Certainties and Doubts*. Montreal: Black Rose Books.

Rapoport, Anatol. 2002. *Skating on Thin Ice*. Oakland, CA: RDR Books.

Rapoport, Anatol, and Albert M. Chammah. 1965. *Prisoner's Dilemma*. Ann Arbor: University of Michigan Press.

Reagan, Ronald. 1983. "Statement on the Death of Herman Kahn." July 8, 1983. https://www.reaganlibrary.gov/archives/speech/statement-death -herman-kahn.

Reid, Walter. 2009. *Architect of Victory: Douglas Haig*. Edinburgh: Birlinn Limited.

Reif, Kingston. 2017. "CBO: Nuclear Arsenal to Cost $1.2 Trillion." Arms Control Association, December 2017. https://www.armscontrol.org/ act/2017-12/news/cbo-nuclear-arsenal-cost-12-trillion.

Riley, Charles. 2015. "Surprise! 260 Million People Live in Just 15 Chinese Cities." *CNN Business*, April 21, 2015. https://money.cnn.com/2015/04/21/ news/economy/china-megacities-population/index.html.

Robinhood. 2021. "Investing for Everyone." https://robinhood.com/us/en.

Robock, Alan. 2010. "Nuclear Winter." *WIREs Climate Change* 1 (May/June): 418–427. http://climate.envsci.rutgers.edu/pdf/WiresClimateChangeNW.pdf.

Rosenbaum, David E. 2004. "The 2004 Campaign: The Independent; Relax, Nader Advises Alarmed Democrats, but the 2000 Math Counsels Otherwise." *The New York Times*, February 24, 2004. https://www .nytimes.com/2004/02/24/us/2004-campaign-independent-relax-nader -advises-alarmed-democrats-but-2000-math.html.

Roth, Alvin. 2015. *Who Gets What—and Why*. New York: Mariner Books.

Roughgarden, Tim. 2016. *Twenty Lectures on Algorithmic Game Theory*. Cambridge: Cambridge University Press.

Royde-Smith, John. 2021. "World War I: Killed, Wounded, and Missing." *Encyclopedia Britannica*, September 28, 2021. https://www.britannica.com/event/World-War-I/Killed-wounded-and-missing.

Royle, Nick J., Per T. Smiseth, and Mathias Kölliker. 2012. *The Evolution of Parental Care*. Oxford: Oxford University Press.

Ruwitch, John. 2021. "China Sends a Record 28 Military Planes into Airspace Controlled by Taiwan." NPR, June 15, 2021. https://www.npr.org/2021/06/15/1006921645/china-sends-a-record-28-military-planes-into-airspace-controlled-by-taiwan.

Ryan, Christopher, and Cacilda Jethá. 2012. *Sex at Dawn*. New York: Harper Perennial.

Sahlins, Marshall. 1972. *Stone-Age Economics*. New York: Aldine Publishing Company. https://www.appropriate-economics.org/materials/Sahlins.pdf.

San Francisco University High School. 2021. "Learning to Love the Atom Bomb: The Cold-War and Sexual Hysteria," accessed September 26, 2021. http://inside.sfuhs.org/dept/history/US_History_reader/Chapter12/learningtolovetheatombomb.html.

Scanes, Colin. 2018. *Animals and Human Society*. London: Academic Press, Elsevier.

Scheidel, Walter. 2017. *The Great Leveler*. Princeton, NJ: Princeton University Press.

Schelling, Thomas. (1960) 1980. *The Strategy of Conflict*. Cambridge, MA: Harvard University Press.

Schelling, Thomas. (1966) 2008. *Arms and Influence*. New Haven, CT: Yale University.

Shapira, Haim. 2017. *Gladiators, Pirates and Games of Trust*. London: Watkins Publishing.

Skyrms, Brian. 2001. "The Stag Hunt." Presidential Address, Pacific Division of the American Philosophical Association, March 2001. https://www.socsci.uci.edu/~bskyrms/bio/papers/StagHunt.pdf.

Sokolski, Henry, ed. 2004. *Getting MAD: Nuclear Mutual Assured Destruction.* Ann Arbor: University of Michigan Library Reprints.

Statista. 2021a. "Largest Cities in Russia 2021." Statista, August 11, 2021. https://www.statista.com/statistics/1090061/largest-cities-in-russia.

Statista. 2021b. "Urbanization in China 1980–2020." Statista, May 12, 2021. https://www.statista.com/statistics/270162/urbanization-in-china.

Statista. 2021c. "Value of Global Equity Trading Worldwide from 1st Quarter 2017 to 2nd Quarter 2021." Statista, September 2021. https://www.statista .com/statistics/242745/volume-of-global-equity-trading.

Stearns, S. C. 1985. "The Evolutionary Significance of Sex." *Experientia* 41, no. 10: 1231–1356. https://stearnslab.yale.edu/sites/default/files/ 16.stearns1985experientia.pdf.

Steiglitz, Ken. 2007. *Snipers, Shills & Sharks: eBay and Human Behavior.* Princeton, NJ: Princeton University Press.

Strauss, Valerie, and Daniel Southerl. 1994. "How Many Died? New Evidence Suggests Far Higher Numbers for the Victims of Mao Zedong's Era." *Washington Post*, July 17, 1994. https://www.washingtonpost.com/archive/ politics/1994/07/17/how-many-died-new-evidence-suggests-far-higher -numbers-for-the-victims-of-mao-zedongs-era/01044df5-03dd-49f4-a453 -a033c5287bce.

Sugden, Robert. 2021. "Hume's Theory of Justice and Vanderschraaf's Vulnerability Objection." *Philosophical Studies* 178: 1719–1729. https://link.springer.com/article/10.1007/s11098-020-01500-4.

Tabrizi, Sharon-Ghamari. 2005. *The Worlds of Herman Kahn.* Cambridge, MA: Harvard University Press.

Tadelis, Steven. 2013. *Game Theory.* Princeton, NJ: Princeton University Press.

Thaler, Richard. 2012. *The Winner's Curse.* New York: Free Press.

Thompson, Nicholas. 2009. "Inside the Apocalyptic Soviet Doomsday Machine." *Wired*, September 21, 2009. https://www.wired.com/2009/09/mf-deadhand.

Toon, O. B., R. P. Turco, A. Robock, C. Bardeen, L. Oman, and G. L. Stenchikov. 2007. "Atmospheric Effects and Societal Consequences of Regional Nuclear Conflicts and Acts of Individual Nuclear Terrorism." *Atmospheric Chemistry and Physics* 7: 1973–2002. https://acp.copernicus.org/articles/7/1973/2007/acp-7-1973-2007.pdf.

Townsend, Quinn. 2020. "Report: The Failed Experiment of Ranked-Choice Voting: A Case Study of Maine and Analysis of 96 Other Jurisdictions." Alaska Policy Forum, October 8, 2020. https://alaskapolicyforum.org/2020/10/failed-experiment-rcv.

Turner, Stansfield. 1997. *Caging the Nuclear Genie*. New York: Westview Press.

Tzu, Sun. 1963. *The Art of War*. Translated by Samuel B. Griffith. Oxford: Oxford University Press.

Vanden Heuvel, Katrina. 2012. "It's Time to End the Electoral College." *The Nation*, November 7, 2012. https://www.thenation.com/article/archive/its-time-end-electoral-college.

VanDerZanden, Ann Marie. 2008. "Reproductive Plant Parts." Oregon State University, January 2008. https://extension.oregonstate.edu/gardening/techniques/reproductive-plant-parts.

Vanguard. 2021. "30-Day Median Bid/Ask Spread." Vanguard Advisors, accessed September 28, 2021. https://advisors.vanguard.com/investments/bidaskspread.

Vickrey, William. 1969. "Tax Simplification through Cumulative Averaging." *Law and Contemporary Problems* 34, no. 4: 736–750. https://core.ac.uk/download/pdf/62555661.pdf.

Vickrey, William. 1996. "Fifteen Fatal Fallacies of Financial Fundamentalism: A Disquisition on Demand Side Economics." Columbia University Working Papers Server Project. http://www.columbia.edu/dlc/wp/econ/vickrey.html.

Vickrey, William. 2021. "Biographical." NobelPrize.org. Nobel Prize Outreach AB 2021, September 28, 2021. https://www.nobelprize.org/prizes/economic-sciences/1996/vickrey/biographical.

Von Clausewitz, Carl. 1993. *On War*. Everyman's Library. Translated by Michael Howard and Peter Paret. New York: Alfred A. Knopf.

Von Neumann, John. 1928. "Zur Theorie der Gesellschaftsspiele (On the Theory of Parlor Games)." *Annals of Mathematics* 100: 295–320. Translated by Sonya Bargmann as "On the Theory of Games of Strategy." https://cs.uwaterloo.ca/~y328yu/classics/vonNeumann.pdf.

Von Neumann, John, and Oskar Morgenstern. (1944) 1953. *Theory of Games and Economic Behavior*. Princeton, NJ: Princeton University Press.

Wallis, W. D. 2014. *The Mathematics of Elections and Voting*. New York: Springer International Publishing.

Weintraub, E. Roy, ed. 1992. *Toward a History of Game Theory*. Durham: Duke University Press.

Wellerstein, Alex. 2021. *Restricted Data: The History of Nuclear Secrecy in the United States*. Chicago: University of Chicago Press.

Whitcomb, Isobel. 2019. "A Nuclear Winter Could Last Years after an All-Out War between Russia and the US." LiveScience, August 30, 2019. https://www.livescience.com/nuclear-winter-disaster.html.

Wilson, Robin. 2008. *Lewis Carroll in Numberland: His Fantastical Mathematical Life*. London: Penguin Books.

Woolf, Jenny. 2010. "Lewis Carroll's Shifting Reputation." *Smithsonian Magazine*, April 2010. https://www.smithsonianmag.com/arts-culture/lewis-carrolls-shifting-reputation-9432378.

Yoon, Carol Caesuk. 2004. "J. Maynard Smith, 84, Dies; Saw Darwinism as Game Theory." *The New York Times*, April 29, 2004. https://www.nytimes.com/2004/04/29/world/j-maynard-smith-84-dies-saw-darwinism-as-game-theory.html.

Zócalo Public Square. 2015. "Women and the Myth of the American West." *Time*, January 11, 2015. https://time.com/3662361/women-american-west.

Notes

Introduction

1. The mathematician Émile Borel wrote several papers during the 1920s that applied calculus and geometry to game theory and proved some special cases of the minimax theorem. But Neumann published a seminal paper in 1928 and subsequently published a 641-page tome, *Theory of Games and Economic Behavior*, in 1944 with the economist Oskar Morgenstern. This book was significantly broader in scope and is considered by most to be the foundational text that established game theory as a formal branch of mathematics.

Chapter 1

1. Genesis 3:5 (New King James Version).

2. It is unclear whether Sun Tzu was an actual person as there is no mention of him in contemporary Chinese histories. There are records of a Sun Bin, possibly a descendant, who wrote several books on military strategy during the fourth century BC.

3. Von Clausewitz (1993), 84.

4. Tzu (1963), vii.

5. This analysis is from Niou et al. (1994).

6. Niou et al. (1994), 172.

7. Recently, a political scientist has coined the term "Thucydides Trap," which refers to a rising state, such as Athens, upsetting the balance of power with an existing hegemon, like Sparta. This theory holds that historically this situation has led to war; the author goes on to draw an analogy with modern-day China and the United States. But the Thucydides Trap is not directly related to game theory.

8. Hume (1740), 520–521.

9. Sugden (2021), 1720.

10. Skyrms (2001), 1.

Chapter 2

1. Biographical background on Neumann is from Macrae (1992) and Poundstone (1992).

2. Chen et al. (2021).

3. It was later translated into English by Sonya Bargmann and published in 1959 under the title "On the Theory of Games of Strategy" in the book *Contributions to the Theory of Games*.

4. Lissner (1946).

5. Weintraub (1992), 115.

6. Biographical background on Nash is from Nasar (2011).

7. Nasar (2011), 11.

8. Nasar (2011), 187.

9. Nasar (2011), 16 and 244.

10. Nasar (2011), 258.

11. Nasar (2011), 292.

12. Kwon (2010).

13. Nash (2021).

14. Holt and Roth (2004).

15. Nasar (2011), 94.

16. See Flood (1952) for a description of the pennies game.

17. Poundstone (1992), 106.

18. Holt and Roth (2004).

19. O'Connor and Robertson (2010).

20. Flood (1952), 18.

21. Flood (1952), 24.

22. Flood (1952), 24.

23. Flood (1952), 24.

Chapter 3

1. Background on Rapoport's life is from Kopelman (2020), Csillag (2007), and Rapoport (2000, 2002).

2. Rapoport (2000), 77.

3. Rapoport (2000), 77.

4. Rapoport (2000), 83.

5. Rapoport (2000), 83.

6. Kopelman (2019), 63.

7. Kopelman (2019), 63.

8. Kopelman (2019), 63.

9. Csillag (2007).

10. Kopelman (2019), 65.

11. Csillag (2007).

12. Rapoport (2000), 89.

13. Rapoport (1960), vii.

14. Rapoport (1960), 232.

15. Rapoport (1960), 220.

16. Rapoport (1960), 220.

17. Rapoport and Chammah (1965), 88.

18. Rapoport and Chammah (1965), 89.

19. Rapoport (1966), 210.

20. Rapoport and Chammah (1965), 36. Rapoport ran various versions of this experiment, but this discussion is limited to what he called the "Pure Matrix" scenario in which the players were given a payoff matrix that showed the benefits of cooperation.

21. Rapoport (2000), 118.

22. Rapoport (2000), 127.

23. Rapoport and Chammah (1965), 191.

24. Rapoport and Chammah (1965), 197.

25. Rapoport and Chammah (1965), viii.

26. Kopelman (2019), 69.

27. Rapoport (1969), xx.

28. Kopelman (2019), 77.

29. Kopelman (2019), 78.

30. Kopelman (2019), 78.

31. See Axelrod (1984), 27–54, for a description of the tournament.

32. Axelrod (1984), 54.

33. Axelrod (1984), 40.

34. See Axelrod (1984), 13–19, for a discussion of the importance of the "shadow of the future." Axelrod's basic idea is that the shadow of the future can be measured by a discount parameter, represented by the variable w. This parameter represents the degree to which the payoff from the next move is discounted relative to the current move. For example, suppose that there is a fifty-fifty chance that a game of prisoner's dilemma will continue to a second move, at which point the game will end. In this instance, the payoff of the second move cannot be more than half the expected value of the payoff from the first move. In addition, the value of a payoff in the future, regardless of the odds of it occurring, is less than the value of a payoff today. One way to measure this further discount is through real interest rates, which reflect the cost of delayed consumption. In fact, we cannot determine the best strategy in a game of prisoner's dilemma without an estimate of the discount parameter w. If the value of w is sufficiently low, then there is never an incentive to cooperate. The extreme case is a value of w equal to zero, the equivalent of a one-move prisoner's dilemma game. But suppose the odds of future rounds are exceptionally low and/or real interest rates are exceptionally high. The shadow of the future may not be dark enough to block out the light from the benefits of defection in the present.

35. See Axelrod (1984), Chapter 4.

36. Axelrod (1984), 78.

37. Axelrod (1984), 80.

38. Axelrod (1984), 79.

39. Axelrod (1984), 81.

40. The discussion of free trade agreements is from Lewis (2011).

41. Lewis (2011), 635.

42. Lewis (2011), 638.

43. Lewis (2011), 649.

44. Macaulay (1963), 60.

45. Macaulay (1963), 62.

46. Macaulay (1963), 61.

47. Macaulay (1963), 61.

48. This example is from Axelrod (1984), 178.

49. Axelrod (1984), 178.

Chapter 4

1. *Humanist News* (2001).

2. Charlesworth (2004).

3. Harper (2004).

4. Nee (2004).

5. Mestel (2004) and Yoon (2004).

6. Maynard Smith (1982), 10.

7. Maynard Smith (1982), 10.

8. Like the instances of TFT we considered, the success in evolutionary terms of a particular behavior depends partly on the behavior of others. Given a fixed number of gazelles, the greater the number of lions within the pride that exhibit aggressive behavior toward this food source, the less the average lion will have to eat.

9. Maynard Smith (1982), 54.

10. Maynard Smith (1982), 54.

11. Maynard Smith (1982), starting on p. 11, analyzes what he calls the hawk-dove game. I have simplified the game for the purposes of this book, but the basic idea is the same.

12. Axelrod (1984), 49.

13. Axelrod (1984), 50.

14. Axelrod (1984), 51.

15. This example is from Poundstone (1992), 248–250.

16. Maynard Smith ([1958] 1975), 195.

17. Greenwood et al. (1985), 179–183.

18. Greenwood et al. (1985), 180.

19. Greenwood et al. (1985), 181.

20. Dawkins (1976), 79–80.

21. Dawkins (1976), 83.

22. This idea is from Dawkins (1976), 80.

23. Dawkins (1976), 81.

24. Dawkins (1976), 232.

25. Merriam-Webster (2021).

26. Dawkins (1976), 141, and Downing (2015).

27. VanDerZanden (2008).

28. Dawkins (1976), 141.

29. Lehtonen (2017).

30. Khan Academy (2021).

31. Diamond (2020).

32. Arney (2021).

33. Maynard Smith ([1958] 1975), 2.

34. Maynard Smith (1978), 3.

35. Engelstädter (2017).

36. Barbuti et al. (2012).

37. Arney (2021).

38. Geary (2021), 27.

39. PBS (2021), 3.

40. PBS (2021), 6.

41. Carroll (1871), s.v. "The Garden of Live Flowers."

42. This phrase and the discussion that follows are based on Dawkins (1976), Chapter 9. I have changed several of the examples and reached different conclusions in places, but the basic ideas are his.

43. This discussion comes from Dawkins (1976), 156–157.

44. Dawkins (1976), 156.

45. Royle et al. (2012), 68.

46. Royle et al. (2012), 72.

47. Royle et al. (2012), 33.

48. Royle et al. (2012), 34.

49. Royle et al. (2012), 34.

50. See Dawkins (1976), Chapter 9.

51. Geary (2021), 36.

52. Geary (2021), 30.

53. Geary (2021), 36.

54. Geary (2021), 130.

55. Greenfeld and Snell (1999).

56. Ryan and Jethá (2012), 68.

57. Ryan and Jethá (2012), 69.

58. Ryan and Jethá (2012), 18.

59. Ryan and Jethá (2012), 63.

60. Hunt (2017).

61. Hunt (2017).

62. Hunt (2017).

63. Gross (2015).

64. Dawkins (1986), 203.

65. Geary (2021), 109.

66. Diamond (2020).

67. Henshaw et al. (2019).

68. Geary (2021), 143.

69. Dawkins (1976), 302.

70. Dunham (2014).

71. Dunham (2014).

72. Enss (2015).

73. Prescott (2007).

74. *Zócalo Public Square* (2015).

75. Furness and Capellini (2019).

76. Furness and Capellini (2019).

77. LeBlanc (2003), 101.

78. Maynard Smith (1978), 10.

Chapter 5

1. Background on Kahn is from Tabrizi (2005), Menand (2005), and Bruce-Briggs (2000).

2. Tabrizi (2005), 62.

3. Tabrizi (2005), 62.

4. Bruce-Briggs (2000), 13.

5. Bruce-Briggs (2000), 24.

6. Tabrizi (2005), 70.

7. Bruce-Briggs (2000), 51.

8. Tabrizi (2005), 77.

9. Tabrizi (2005), 75.

10. Menand (2005).

11. Bruce-Briggs (2000), 280.

12. Bruce-Briggs (2000), 267.

13. Bruce-Briggs (2000), 270.

14. Reagan (1983).

15. After this first book, Kahn never actually wrote another. His colleagues would record and edit his lectures and conversations, then present the results to Kahn, and he would sign his name.

16. Kaplan (2004).

17. Kahn (1960a).

18. San Francisco University High School (2021).

19. Turner (1997), 8.

20. Turner (1997), 12.

21. Abella (2008), 159.

22. Abella (2008), 90.

23. Keller (2013).

24. Bruce-Briggs (2000), 110.

25. Bruce-Briggs (2000), 114.

26. Abella (2008), 103.

27. Jervis (2002).

28. Kahn (1984), 41.

29. Gavin (2020), 199.

30. Gavin (2020), 199.

31. Davenport and Reif (2020).

32. Davenport and Reif (2020).

33. Davenport and Reif (2020).

34. Kahn (1965), 9.

35. Kahn (1965), 10.

36. Kahn (1965), 10.

37. Kahn (1965), 14.

38. Kahn (1965).

39. Bruce-Briggs (2000), 120.

40. Bruce-Briggs (2000), 93.

41. Bruce-Briggs (2000), 94.

42. Bruce-Briggs (2000), 94.

43. Description of Perimeter is from Ellsberg (2017) and Hoffman (2009).

44. Thompson (2009).

45. Ellsberg (2017), 306.

46. Thompson (2009).

47. Abella (2008), 161.

48. Abella (2008), 161.

49. As recounted in Ellsberg (2017), 62–63, Secretary of Defense Robert McNamara during the Kennedy administration was concerned about a rogue US commander starting World War III. In 1962, McNamara ordered electronic locks placed on Minutemen missiles, requiring the local commanders to enter an eight-digit code from a higher authority before launching a missile. However, the Air Force generals chafed at this restriction and, unbeknownst to McNamara, set all codes to 00000000. The codes were not changed for almost another twenty years.

50. Bruce-Briggs (2000), 87.

51. Whitcomb (2019) and Brasch (2020).

52. Toon et al. (2007).

53. Robock (2010).

54. Toon et al. (2007).

55. Robock (2010).

56. Earth Institute at Columbia University (2020).

57. Even without the impact of a nuclear winter, one study concluded that an attack of 250 warheads on the US mainland would kill 60 percent of the population within two years from a breakdown of the nation's ability to house, clothe, and feed itself. Gross domestic product would remain at about 25 percent of prewar levels for twenty years. This study also concluded that 250 warheads dropped on the Russian and Chinese homelands would have a similar impact. (See Turner [1997], 138–144).

58. Gavin (2020), 182.

59. Kahn (1960a), 18.

60. Kahn (1960a), 14.

61. Kahn (1960a), 14.

62. Kahn (1960a), 35.

63. Bruce-Briggs (2000), 108.

64. Lieber and Press (2020), 101.

65. I believe the odds of a full-scale first strike by Russia are now significantly less than during the Cold War. Sixty years ago, Soviet planners may have envisioned scenarios in which they could "win" a nuclear war with the United States by taking out most of our missiles. Today, the fact that a global winter will follow a full-scale first strike completely alters that calculation. In addition, the Soviet Union in 1960 was ruled with an iron fist by the Communist Party. Fifteen years earlier, the Soviet Union lost more than sixteen million people, or 15 percent of its population, in a war with Germany. A nuclear war may have been seriously considered by the dogmatic, austere Soviet dictators of that time who could rationalize the loss of tens of millions more people as an acceptable price to pay to free the working classes of the world by defeating the capitalists who had killed millions of their brothers and sons during World War II. Today, a politically agnostic, kleptocratic Russian leadership depends on the support of the Russian people, for whom World War II is a distant memory and an economy freed from corruption is still a stretch goal.

66. Gavin (2020), 116.

67. Lieber and Press (2020), 113.

68. Lieber and Press (2020), 113.

69. Turner (1997), 78.

70. Strauss and Southerl (1994).

71. Ruwitch (2021).

72. *Moscow Times* (2018).

73. Statista (2021a).

74. Statista (2021b).

75. Riley (2015).

76. Lieber and Press (2020), 11.

77. Lieber and Press (2020), 71.

78. Lieber and Press (2020), 71.

79. Lieber and Press (2020), 71.

80. Lieber and Press (2020), 71.

81. Lieber and Press (2020), 71.

82. Reif (2017).

83. ICAN (2019).

84. Data on US nuclear forces is from Kristensen and Korda (2021).

85. Davenport and Reif (2020).

86. Grady (2021).

87. This assumes nations and their leaders are rational. It is possible that a country could be irrationally committed to the destruction of another, even at the cost of its own survival. I believe this is not the case today and for the foreseeable future for the United States, China, and Russia. One can worry about other countries, such as Iran, which has publicly committed to the destruction of the State of Israel and whose religious leaders may not be constrained by self-preservation.

88. Quote Investigator (2012).

Chapter 6

1. Background on Haig is from Reid (2009).

2. Anderton and Carter (2019), 180.

3. Royde-Smith (2021).

4. Farnam Street Media (2017).

5. Farnam Street Media (2017).

6. Norman (2007).

7. Reid (2009), kindle version: location 4772.

8. Reid (2009), kindle version: location 5024.

9. Quote Investigator (2012).

10. Pinker (2012) makes this argument on pp. 78–80.

Chapter 7

1. Biographical details about Dodgson are from Poundstone (2008), Douglas-Fairhurst (2015), Wilson (2008), and Leach (2015).

2. Poundstone (2008), 153.

3. Douglas-Fairhurst (2015), 425.

4. Leach (1996).

5. Poundstone (2008), 151.

6. McLean et al. (1996), 26.

7. Woolf (2010).

8. Quinn (2018).

9. Knifton (2020).

10. Knifton (2020).

11. Douglas-Fairhurst (2015), 132.

12. Leach (2005).

13. Leach (1996).

14. Douglas-Fairhurst (2015), 132.

15. Kennedy (2001).

16. Poundstone (2008), 160.

17.   McLean et al. (1996), 12.

18.   The actual method behind ending the "cycle" is more complicated, but this is the basic idea.

19.   Poundstone (2008), 160.

20.   Townsend (2020).

21.   Another possible scenario is that an increase in support for a candidate leads to a worse outcome, what game theorists call "non-monotonicity." This can occur under instant runoff voting when support for the three candidates is more evenly divided, and preferences are not aligned with parties. But the conditions for non-monotonicity to occur must be just right. Voters have to be about evenly split in their support for the candidates, and the supporters of the second-place candidate must switch just the right amount of their support to the first-place candidate. In an election with two clear front-runners and several more fringe candidates, non-monotonicity is rarely an issue.

22.   This account and discussion about Arrow are from Poundstone (2008). Poundstone interviewed Arrow before he died and highlighted for the first time (for many people) the important contributions of his work.

23.   Poundstone (2008), 42.

24.   Poundstone (2008), 42.

25.   Arrow (1948), 3.

26.   McKenna (2008).

27.   Dieter (2003).

28.   Dieter (2003).

29.   Herron and Lewis (2006).

30.   Rosenbaum (2004).

31.   Kurrild-Klitgaard (2016).

32.   Kurrild-Klitgaard (2016).

33. Hotelling (1929), 54.

34. All this assumes voter turnout is not a factor. But including this variable complicates the analysis without adding to the comparison between voting systems.

35. Cooper and Munger (2000), 351.

36. Cooper and Munger (2000).

37. Cooper and Munger (2000), 338.

38. Cooper and Munger (2000), 338.

39. Cooper and Munger (2000), 337.

40. Cooper and Munger (2000), 338.

41. National Archives (2021).

42. Vanden Heuvel (2012).

43. National Conference of State Legislatures (2020).

Chapter 8

1. Drèze (1998), 407.

2. Vickrey (2021).

3. Vickrey (2021).

4. Beyer (1992).

5. Beyer (1992).

6. Drèze (1998), 406.

7. *Columbia University Record* (1997).

8. Drèze (1998), 414.

9. Drèze (1998), 416.

10. *Columbia University Record* (1997).

11. Vickrey (1969).

12. Vickrey (1996).

13. In theory, auctions could also be based on third, fourth, or any higher-numbered price, but beyond a second price, there would not be an incentive for a seller to do so if auctioning a single item.

14. Steiglitz (2007), 19.

15. Fine (2021).

16. Fine (2021).

17. Nicas (2017).

18. eBay (2021a).

19. McCormick (2021).

20. McCormick (2021).

21. Google (2021).

22. eBay (2018).

23. In the case where the highest bid price is less than the second bid price plus the bidding increment, then the highest bid price is displayed.

24. Steiglitz (2007), 43.

25. Steiglitz (2007), 45.

26. eCommerce Bytes (2017).

27. eBay (2021b).

28. Dummies (2016).

29. Steiglitz (2007), 122.

30. Capen et al. (1971).

31. Capen et al. (1971), 641.

32. Capen et al. (1971), 641.

33. Capen et al. (1971), 652.

34. Gardner (2003), 316.

35. Gardner (2003), 316.

36. Steiglitz (2007), 138.

37. Banks (2004), 120.

38. Brenner et al. (2007).

39. Statista (2021c).

40. Vanguard (2021).

41. Abdi and Ranaldo (2017).

42. Robinhood (2021).

43. Robinhood (2021).

44. Osipovich (2021).

Index

About the Author

DAVID LOCKWOOD is a former lecturer on the faculty of the Graduate School of Business at Stanford University. He has three decades of experience as a senior executive in Silicon Valley and has served on more than twenty public and private company boards. In addition, he has been a senior advisor to the US government on nuclear and energy issues.